HERMETIC SCIENCE

OF

MOTION AND NUMBER

By
Dr. A. S. Raleigh
Late Official Scribe Of The Hermetic Brotherhood

A Course of Private Lessons

DeVorss & Company
Box 550
Marina del Rey, California 90291

FOREWORD.

In these twelve lessons there is presented to the student a perfect knowledge of the Science of Motion. He will in this way be able to perfectly understand the ultimate, as well as the immediate cause of all manifestation of nature. In this way the first steps toward an understanding of the Theosophia will be taken. Without this knowledge, an understanding of nature in the abstract is an utter impossibility.

TABLE OF CONTENTS.

CONTENTS

LESSON I.

The Law of Motion.

ALL things in the material world are the result of motion. The doctrine as laid down by John Tyndall, that all things are a mode of motion of force, is perfectly true. It is simply the reappearing of the ancient metaphysics. Tyndall adopted the theory from Schopenhauer, Schopenhauer adopted it from Kant, and Kant obtained it from the Neoplatonists, and they secured it from Pythagoras; Pythagoras learned it in Egypt and India. It becomes, therefore, the universal conception of the occult scientists of the ancient world. It is the key to the constitution of matter in relation to force.

The MODERN chemist is coming to discover the truth of a number of those things which were held and taught by the ancient alchemists. We are beginning to learn that the so-called elements are not really simple elements; but are in reality mere combinations. We were taught some years ago that there were seventy-two elements, which were absolutely elementary and could not be divided. We have found, however, that there are eighty-six so far located as so-called elements, but none of them are really elements. They are simply combinations.

THE MOLECULE.

The molecule is the unit of the element. The element can not be divided without the dissolution of the molecule. Physical change consists in the division of any substance in a

1

group of matter into its constituent molecules. Chemical change consists in the division of the molecule into its component atoms.

THE ATOM.

There are only four kinds of atoms; all the others are mere molecules. The four elements of the old alchemists, were:

> earth,
> air,
> fire and
> water,

or in modern parlance,

> carbon,
> nitrogen,
> oxygen and
> hydrogen.

These are the basis from which the so-called elements of chemistry are formed. The molecule is simply a structure formed of the combination of these four atoms.

ALCHEMICAL CHANGE.

The alchemical *change* which the old alchemists were trying to accomplish, was the division of these four atoms into the ULTIMATE PHYSICAL ATOM from which they were formed. When we have passed back of these, we come to the Ultimate physical atom, or the etheric atom, which is the basis of formation, of the generation of the four atoms.

ULTIMATE ATOMS.

There are three ultimate atoms: The ultimate PHYSICAL atom, which is the unit of ether; the ultimate VITAL or ASTRAL atom, which is the unit of life force; and the ultimate MENTAL atom, which is the unit of MIND. These three are the basis of those three primates, of which all things are formed. But the three primates themselves are structures formed from the one primary cosmic energy, the unit of which is the ULTIMATE atom.

VIBRATION.

All forms of energy are in a continuous state of vibration. The cosmic energy, with its ultimate atom, is vibrating to a certain rhythm. This rhythm holds the energy of the atom together. The atom, by reason of this rhythm, assumes a certain form—a definite geometrical figure. It also expresses itself in a definite color and produces a definite sound, by reason of its rhythmic vibration.

RHYTHM.

When the RATE of vibration has fallen below a certain point, the rhythm of mind is reached—that is to say, the ULTIMATE atom begins to vibrate in accordance with the rhythm of the MENTAL plane. When this takes place, the various atoms which are vibrating to this rhythm are, by reason of the rhythm, attracted and held together by cohesion. The rhythm of MIND governs and controls this ultimate mental atom. These atoms differ in accordance with the different rhythms, or notes, which govern the vibration of the mental plane. Thus, they are drawn together and form in accordance with the rhythm, or note, which is governing the vibration. When the vibration or rhythm, descends below the level of the mental plane, the highest vibration is on a scale lower than the lowest vibration of the mental scale, and the rhythm of life is the result. When the rhythm of life is established within the atom, the mental atom is dissolved into its constituent ultimate atoms. The rhythm of life is now established within them, so they vibrate in accordance with that rhythm. They are thus drawn together by attraction, bound by cohesion, the result being the ULTIMATE VITAL or ASTRAL atom.

This atom, vibrating now in accordance with the rhythm of LIFE, being held together by this NOTE, assumes a form in accordance with its quality and rate of vibration. It also produces a color corresponding to it.

By a HIGH rate of vibration, we mean a rapid, intense vibration; also a short wave-length vibration. By a LOW rate of vibration, we mean a correspondingly slower vibration, more gradual, and also a correspondingly longer wave-length vibration.

ULTIMATE PHYSICAL ATOM.

When the SCALE of vibration has descended to that point where the highest vibration is on a scale lower than the lowest vibration of the vital or astral scale, the atom is again dissolved into its constituent ultimate atoms. These ultimate atoms begin to vibrate in accordance with the physical rhythm or etheric rhythm, and by reason of this rhythm are drawn together and held by cohesion, thus forming the ultimate PHYSICAL atom, which is held together by the physical note or rhythm of the physical plane. This ultimate physical atom is the unit of ether. All matter vibrating upon this highest subdivision of the physical scale, which has for its unit the ultimate physical atom, is etheric.

The physical atoms, by reason of this rate of vibration, travel in STRAIGHT lines back and forth. The mental atoms, by reason of their rhythm travel in ZIGZAG lines. The astral atoms—that is to say, the atoms of emotion, feeling, desire—travel in a CURVED line, while the LIFE vibrations of the astral atom travel in a SPIRAL.

Thus in the various forces of nature, these various forms of energy in their vibratory activity, not only assume a definite form, but also travel each in a definite direction, pertaining to itself alone. In the formation of organisms, therefore, the character of the energy determines, by reason of its peculiar direction of activity, the figure of the object.

GENESIS OF THE ATOMS.

When the *ultimate physical atoms* descend one step in the rate of vibration, they combine by reason of the lower vibration being held together by cohesion, forming the ELECTRON of electricity, which electron being the unit of electricity, is the second sub-plane of the etheric or physical plane, the pure ether being the first. Descending one step lower, the vibration draws together the atoms by cohesion and forms the electron of MAGNETISM, which electron is the unit of magnetism, being the third sub-plane of the physical plane. Descending still lower in its rate of vibration, the electrical electron differentiates itself. First: Into the positive electric, or fire atoms, the fire atom being the same as the *oxygen*, only of an etheric rather than a gaseous form. Second: Into the negative electric, or water atom, which is the same as the atom of *hydrogen*, only being etheric rather than gaseous.

Each of these atoms has its own particular chord which binds together and holds the various electrons by cohesion, so as to form its atomic structure—the atom being merely a structure formed of electrons. The electrons of magnetism, descending one step lower in the vibratory scale, vibrate to another chord which binds together and holds them by cohesion, forming the POSITIVE magnetic, or EARTH atom, the same as the modern atom of *carbon*. The magnetic electron descending still further in its vibratory rate, a number of them are drawn together by reason of the lower chord, and held by cohesion, forming the NEGATIVE magnetic, or AIRY atom, the same as the modern chemical atom of *nitrogen*.

THE SEX PRINCIPLE IN NATURE.

The ELECTRICAL FORCE is the *masculine* force of nature; the MAGNETIC is the *feminine*. It is by reason of this sex differentiation that the physical world is able to be produced from the ether. This principle was clearly understood by the ancient Greeks when they taught the birth of the world from FATHER ETHER.

It will be seen, therefore, that far from being a mere animal condition for the sake of carnal gratification, SEX differentiation exists in the very foundation of nature. The manifested universe could have no *existence* without it. It is by the UNION of the two principles—electricity and magnetism—each positively and negatively differentiating, so as to form the four elementaries—OXYGEN, HYDROGEN, NITROGEN and CARBON— otherwise earth, air, fire and water—that the chemical world has been produced.

PERSONIFICATION OF THE ELEMENTS.

We can now, in the light of this, understand why all nations of antiquity have personified fire and water, the electrical elements by GODS in the MALE form, and the earth and air by GODDESSES in the FEMALE form, because they are magnetic, therefore, FEMININE in their genesis.

GENESIS OF THE MOLECULE.

The atoms of these four elementaries by combination, form the various molecules of the eighty-six chemical elements; the character of these elements depends upon the proportion in which the four elements are united, each element contributing its rate of vibration chord, in accordance with the proportion in which it is present in the combination—that is to say, the number of its atoms which are present in proportion to the atoms of the other elements, each atom moving in accordance with the rate of vibration, the CHORD governing its vibratory activity; the various CHORDS being drawn together, cause them to act harmoniously, blending to form a certain TONE. This tone binds together and holds the atoms, both by ADHESION and COHESION, so as to form the molecule, and the molecule depends for its character upon the tone which holds it together.

THE KEYNOTE.

There are eighty-six different vibratory TONES which, therefore, give rise to eighty-six different kinds of molecules, and hence, to eighty-six different chemical elements. When these various molecules combine, by reason of a *keynote* which holds them together, causing the various *tones* to BLEND and UNITE, it produces the harmonious rhythmic force with *one dominant* note, constituting the KEYNOTE, the note which binds and holds all the others together, preserving their unity through adhesion and cohesion, and a physical object is produced. Every group of matter—mineral or organic—is merely a structure composed of numberless molecules of the various chemical elements held together by a KEYNOTE.

We can see from this that everything in the material world

is nothing but the result of vibration. The very form, the very substance, socalled, which we look at and take for reality, is nothing but a FORTUITOUS CONCOURSE OF ATOMS, as Professor Haeckel would call it, and this fortuitous councourse of atoms is nothing but the outgrowth of a HARMONIOUS STATE OF VIBRATION.

GENESIS OF FORM.

The whole secret of the constitution of matter is therefore, this: All form is merely a mode of motion of force, and force itself is but a mode of motion of the original cosmic energy. In fact, form is found on all the planes of nature, the forms present in the finer forces simply combining to form the more gross forms on the lower planes of nature.

This is the secret of the philosophy of Kant, Berkeley and Schopenhauer, which teaches that the *material world* is only an *illusion;* the *ideal world* is the reality, the *physical* world is but an illusion. It is also the secret underlying the Vedanta philosophy and those various philosophies of India, denying the reality of the material world, teaching it to be but an ILLUSION OF THE SENSES.

We look at a block of marble, for instance; it appears to us to be solid. We think, here is reality, truly here is substance. We speak of this as being something tangible, something real, the other things, idealism, etc., being visionary. A greater mistake was never made. This block of marble which we regard as being so real, so substantial, is in truth merely millions of molecules, *relatively* as far apart as the earth is from the sun, which are revolving around each other, vibrating about one another; and only held together by reason of the KEYNOTE which binds together and unifies all the various tones, chords, notes, rhythms, vibrations, etc.

UNREALITY OF MATTER.

Were it not for the intense rapidity of this vibration, we would be able to see the unreality of the object. The only reason why it appears to be solid, firm, substantial, is because its molecules are vibrating so rapidly we cannot see them. Were the keynote to cease, were a force to be introduced sufficient to break the power of this keynote—the binding power—immediately the block of marble would be dissolved into its constituent molecules, they would each and all go off on a tangent; the force which preserves the equilibrium and binds the molecules together having ceased to act, the object would disappear.

ILLUSION.

We can see, therefore, that a physical object is merely the result of the HARMONIOUS VIBRATION OF THE MOLECULES of which it is composed; consequently it has no *permanent* reality. It is merely the result of vibration, the result is observed by the senses, but the vibration, which is the substance—that which is the foundation on which the object stands—this vibration cannot be seen because of the grossness of the physical senses, while as a matter of fact it is the *only* reality; it is THE CAUSE, the object is the EFFECT.

It is because of this fact that the idealistic philosophers have always denominated the physical world, *the world of illusion*. It is an illusion because it is not what it seems to be—an illusion of the senses. Because of this fact, the Vedantins have always taken the position that the material world was nothing but a mode of motion of the ether; therefore, the ether is the only reality. This was also the doctrine of Kant and others, but only this; Sankaracharya realized that the ETHERIC SELF, as well as the LIFE and MIND, even, are but mode of motion of the COSMIC ENERGY—the INNER akasha of the Hindus; therefore, these are all illusions; they are not reality; they are not what they seem to be, but are merely modes of motion of the cosmic energy, and, therefore, they are an illusion of the senses; they have no existence in themselves, in the ABSOLUTE, but only in the RELATIVE. This was also understood by Buddha, when he taught there was nothing but akasha and Nirvana, or as we say in the West, vibration, merely modes of motion of these two forces.

THE REAL.

But Sankaracharya and Shri Krishna go still a step further, and they tell us that as a matter of fact AKASHA, the COSMIC ENERGY itself, is merely a mode of motion, merely a rate of vibration of NIRVANA or SPIRIT; and we can go still further, for Sankaracharya goes still further and shows us that SPIRIT itself is but vibration, a mode of motion from PARABRAHMAN, GOD, the ABSOLUTE, and therefore, there is NOTHING ELSE BUT GOD; it is but an illusion of the senses; there nothing exists but GOD: This outer world is but a world of form which is merely the manifestation—the outer expression, the shadow, the reflection of GOD, PARA-BRAHMAN, THE UNMANIFEST; therefore, he denies that they have any existence. To him they are merely illusions of the senses. They are not things in themselves, but are merely appearances. We see them, we think they are real because we do not realize that they are but manifestations, but expressions, but forms which the DIVINE ENERGY assumes in its manifestations—merely a mask which conceals the DIVINE ENERGY which is back of all these things. They are only expressions of the phenomenal world, and not the NOU-MENAL—things as they seem and not things as they are.

For this reason, the oriental teachers deny the personality, deny all expressions and appearances, and try to realize the nothingness of the world in order that they may comprehend the REALITY. It is not that they deny that the outer things exist in the sense in which a Westerner would deny it. They do not deny that the thing exists in the relative. What they deny, is that it exists in the ABSOLUTE, as a thing in ITSELF.

The whole purpose of this attitude is the recognition, that all these objects which are presented to the senses are merely the result of the co-operative, harmonious activity of motion as presented to the physical senses, and the appearance, which it assumes is simply because of the limitation of our physical senses, because they are unable to penetrate to the reality, recognize the force of motion which is back of, underlying and expressing itself in and through the form.

They affirm the ILLUSION of form because it is a mere appearance, a limitation, the RESULT of a view of the various molecules, etc., collectively, and not individually. It is in this sense, in the sense of it being a limited view, instead of a complete view, that they affirm the ILLUSORY CHARACTER of the PHYSICAL world, and in this they are right. It is in this sense an illusion of the senses; it is merely a projection, a manifestation, which is the outgrowth of motion, according to NUMBER in all the various combinations, as stated in the foregoing.

UNKNOWABLE.

This gives the KEY to the CONSTITUTION OF MATTER and its relation to FORCE. It is in this way, by a perfect system of scales, etc., that we are able to understand the RISING and MANIFESTATION OF FORCE into matter, the evolution of FORM, and all these principles which the scientists generally relegate to the realm of the UNKNOWABLE, because they do not know anything of them themselves, and they assume, therefore, that it is impossible to understand them.

Ever since science accepted the dictum of Herbert Spencer, that the Absolute is totally inexplicable; that the mind cannot form the slightest comprehension of things in themselves, but can only comprehend the relative, all effort for the attainment of ULTIMATE knowledge has been abandoned. Starting out with the assumption that knowledge is received through the physical senses, this view is perfectly consistent.

But there is a realm beyond the border which can never be penetrated by the physical senses. Man has been provided with a set of metaphysical senses for the cognition of this realm of nature. The facts cognized by these senses, are just as much facts as those cognized through the physical senses. When the intellectual faculties derive all their facts from the physical world, they can only arrive at physical conclusions; for the intellect can only reason from data, and as the data is, so will be the conclusion. Even in the case of deductive reasoning, the effect must correspond to the cause which is taken as the premise from which the deduction is made.

It will be seen, therefore, that without data concerning the metaphysical realm, it will be an utterly impossible feat to attain unto a knowledge of metaphysical truths by the reason.

What we require is an induction based upon all the PHENOMENA OF NATURE, both physical and metaphysical, leading to the principles which will be universal, and may be taken as a basis for deduction which will lead unto universal effects, thus enabling us to reach NOUMENA, and not merely phenomena. In this way we will have a real SCIENCE, and not merely a physical philosophy.

With this science of Cosmology, there must be correlated a perfectly scientific knowledge of man in all of his parts dealing with all of the principles, the unseen and occult, as well as the seen and tangible. The latent powers of the Soul must be considered and assigned their proper place, as well as all of the present known psychic faculties. In this way a perfect and complete psychology, dealing with the entire constitution of man must be formulated and correlated with the science of Cosmology above described.

Together with this, there must be correlated a science of Divinity, resting not upon speculative philosophy dealing with the testimony of another, credulity or human opinion, but upon individual interior illumination. Our view of God must rest solely upon personal experience, upon an individual union with him, resulting in a personal acquaintance with HIM. It must be a matter of absolute knowledge, not mere belief. Such a knowledge of God, resting upon individual enlightenment and not upon testimony no matter how reliable, will constitute a true Theosophia (divine wisdom) rather than a theologia (divine knowledge). This is the true meaning of THEOSOPHY in its narrower sense, and only those who have this Divine Wisdom are Theosophists in the true sense.

When this Theosophy is correlated with the psychology and the Cosmology above described, we will have a complete science showing the relation between God, man and the universe, and at the same time, containing nothing but absolute truth. In this way the road to ultimate knowledge, or more properly speaking, WISDOM, in relation to all things, both natural and divine, is opened. And this is the meaning of Theosophy in the broader sense of the term.

NATURE being but a manifestation of GOD, Theosophy (divine wisdom) must in the ultimate include the relation of nature, the effect, to God, the cause.

The various Theosophical societies have reduced Theosophy to a philosophical cult, and have thus destroyed its character of a science, or rather of the Divine Wisdom. True

Theosophy has nothing to do one way or the other with the theories which these societies have falsely put forward under the sacred name of Theosophy.

The Divine Wisdom in the sense above stated is what we teach in these lessons. We, therefore, teach everything, but only absolute truth, in regard to every subject, giving the relation between God, man and the universe, and only giving out first hand knowledge on each point so dealt with.

As an introduction to the study of this Theosophia, it is necessary that we have an understanding of the ultimate constitution of nature. In order to accomplish this end, the Science of Motion and Number, or true metaphysics, must be understood. This science gives the ultimate cause of all the phenomena of nature. It is in a word, a kind of transcendental physics, dealing with the unseen, as well as the seen. The first requisite, therefore, to an understanding of Theosophia is an understanding of the Science of Motion and Number.

LESSON II.

The Law of Opposites.

The ten pairs of opposites of Pythagoras were:

    1st: Right and left.
    2nd: Even and odd.
    3rd: Hot and cold.
    4th: Hard and soft.
    5th: Light and darkness.
    6th: Male and female.
    7th: Good and evil.
    8th: Stationary and movable.
    9th: Square and oblong.
    10th: Wet and dry.

Within these ten pairs of opposites, is contained the entire law of opposites in all of its variations.

As was stated in the first lesson, the ultimate physical atoms of ether, by combination become the electrons of electricity and magnetism according to the rate of vibration with which they move, magnetism being one rate lower in the vibratory scale than electricity. Everything in the material world is merely the result of the combination of these two principles.

Not only this, but the vital and mental atoms are also differentiated in some way into two forces analogous to electricity and magnetism. In fact, on all the planes of nature we find this twofold force manifesting itself and being the law and cause of all activity. The electric is the masculine principle and the magnetic the feminine principle of nature.

15

In man the brain is sexed, the left hemisphere being the seat of the electrical force, and the right hemisphere the seat of the magnetic force. This is true of all the various principles in man. The nerves from the left hemisphere of the brain pass over to the right side of the body, thus making a cross as they pass from the brain to the body. Thus it is that while the left side of the brain is the electrical center, it governs the right side of body, likewise the right side of the brain, the magnetic center, governs the left side of the body.

It is because of a realization of this principle that artists, when painting a portrait to represent strength, dignity, grandeur, courage, nobility and force, all masculine attributes, paint the right side of the face. While if they wish to represent beauty, ideality, purity, gentleness, meekness and affection, all feminine attributes, they paint the left side of the face. And this is true, although they know nothing of the great sexual law.

The outward effects of this law are so prominent that they may be easily noted by anyone. For the same reason the man walks on the right, the woman on the left, thus recognizing the true position as the electrical and magnetic personality. Even the sex organs of the man are largely on the right side of the body, likewise those of the female are largely on the left side.

The electrical force goes down the right arm and out through the right hand, making it the channel through which the electrical force escapes. The magnetic force goes down through the left arm and out through the left hand, making that the channel through which the magnetic force escapes. In healing, electricity passes through the right hand and magnetism through the left hand. For this reason the right hand has become emblematic of the electrical force of nature and the left hand of the magnetic force of nature. By right and left is therefore meant the electrical and magnetic forces of the nature out of which all things in the material world are produced. And as electricity and magnetism are merely different rates of vibration, it follows that right and left are also only different rates of vibration.

EVEN AND ODD.

Even represents those conditions where the electrical and magnetic forces are evenly balanced, where the equilibrium is perfectly maintained, while on the other hand, odd represents those conditions where one of the above principles greatly predominates over the other, so as to make the object, substance or principle, as the case may be, prominently and distinctly electrical or magnetic.

Even also represents the state where the keynote is weak, and as a result, the molecules are held together in loose affinity, while odd represents the state where the keynote is strong, so that the molecules are bound together in close affinity. When anything is even, the affinity is easily destroyed, and it is easily separated into its component molecules, atoms, electrons, etc. When it is odd, the affinity is with difficulty destroyed, and it is therefore, difficult to separate it into its component molecules, atoms, electrons, etc.

As the electrical and magnetic forces are merely matters of vibration, the proportion of each which may be present is merely a question of the proportion of the two rates of vibration. And as the affinity and the keynote are alike matters of vibration, deriving their strength and power from the intensity of the vibration, the whole matter is merely a question of vibration. Even and odd, therefore, represent merely rates of vibration and different states of combination in the electrical and magnetic forces.

HOT AND COLD.

John Tyndall has shown that heat is merely a mode of motion, or in other words, molecular vibration. When the molecules reach a certain point in the intensity of their vibration they become hot and then the higher their rate of vibration, the hotter they become. It, therefore, appears that heat is merely a certain rate of vibration. The mistake which scientists here make, however, is in denying the reality of cold, calling it merely the absence of heat. Cold is no more the absence of heat than heat is the absence of cold. Heat being the result of a certain rate of vibration, cold is the result of the absence of that rate of vibration. As inertia exists nowhere, this rate of vibration is absent because another rate of vibration is present. Cold is, therefore, a mode of motion, a rate of vibration, quite as much as heat. All vibrations of electricity are hot; all vibrations of magnetism are cold.

The dividing line between heat and cold is, therefore, the point at which electricity becomes magnetism. This is not only true of the physical plane, but also of the vital and mental, the buddhic and spiritual. Wherever we go we find that the magnetic is cold and the more magnetic it becomes, the colder it becomes; the electric is hot and the more electric it becomes, the hotter it becomes.

Heat and cold are, therefore, merely the effect of the electrical and magnetic forces of nature in their vibratory activity. It must be borne in mind that this remark applies to all the principles of man and nature as well as to the physical.

In heating matter we merely raise the vibration so as to produce the degree of heat which we desire. By so doing, we make it electrical. As water freezes, its vibration is continually lowered and thus it becomes magnetic. A hot bath is always electrical, while a cold bath is always magnetic. Take a person who is intensely magnetic and give him a hot bath and it will draw off the superabundance of magnetism, at the same time giving off to his body a quantity of electricity; will restore the equilibrium and in this way be most beneficial.

On the other hand, let an intensely electrical person take a hot bath, and the bath will draw off a part of his already diminished magnetism, at the same time giving him still more electricity, so as to make the unbalanced condition still worse and will be, therefore, most injurious, and if persisted in long enough, will cause death; for life is the result of the balancing of the two forces.

In the same way let a strongly electrical person take a cold bath and the magnetic bath will draw off the superabundance of the electrical force, at the same time giving to him a part of its magnetism, thus tending to establish equilibrium, and will in this way, be most beneficial. On the other hand, let an intensely magnetic person take a cold bath and the magnetic water will draw off some of his already depleted electrical force, and at the same time give to him still more magnetic force, tending still more to overturn the equilibrium.

In this case, it will prove most injurious, and if persisted in long enough, will result in death. This is the reason why hydropaths so often kill their patients. They will put an electrical patient into a hot bath; or a magnetic patient into a cold bath, and thus they are wrecked, whereas had they placed the electrical patient into a cold bath, and the magnetic patient into a hot bath, they would have been greatly benefited.

No person should ever attempt to practice hydropathy without an understanding of this law of polarity and also the ability to diagnose the electrical and magnetic condition of his patient. This all applies equally to the thermal treatment, to electrotherapeutics and to animal magnetism. Heat and cold are therefore, merely another name for electricity and magnetism.

HARD AND SOFT.

As all substances are merely a collection of molecules held together by affinity, resulting from the harmony of their vibration, the closer the affinity is, the more intense the vibration, the harder it becomes to displace the molecules owing to the tenacity with which they adhere and cohere one to the other. In this case the substance becomes hard, because of the strength of its keynote, the intensity of its vibration, and the closeness of its affinity.

On the other hand, the looser the affinity, the lower the rate of vibration, the more easy it becomes to displace the molecules owing to the laxity with which they adhere and cohere one to another. In this case the substance becomes soft, because of the weakness of its keynote, the lowness of its rate of vibration, and the looseness of its affinity.

Hardness and softness are, therefore, different states of affinity growing out of different states of the vibratory activity; of the constituent molecules of the substance. Hardness is therefore, merely another name for close affinity, and softness for loose affinity. The only difference is therefore a difference of vibration.

LIGHT AND DARKNESS.

Light is a mode of motion, a rate of vibration. In the pure ether all is darkness. It is only when ether is differentiated into electricity and magnetism that light appears. As electricity and magnetism are different rates of vibration from ether, therefore light is a different rate of vibration from darkness. Darkness is not the absence of light any more than light is the absence of darkness. They are each merely the effect of different rates of vibration. All was darkness before the light vibration was imparted to the ether, causing the light to be born out of the darkness. For out of night was born the day. Remember light is one rate of vibration and darkness the other, and that is the only absolute and ultimate distinction between the two.

MALE AND FEMALE.

The male is the embodiment of the electrical principle. His sex organs are the means through which the electric force is manifested. Not only this, but the entire bodily form is a physical expression of this principle. Not only is the electric principle expressed through the physical body, but the life, the emotional nature, and the mind as well as the soul and the spirit show forth the electrical principle in all of their activities.

Thus we can see the fallacy of the assertion that sex is only of the body. All the principles of man are sexed. Not only are the principles of man, but also the seven principles are alike sexed. Sex lies at the very foundation of the constitution of matter. Not only is it present in all form, but also in the very principles of nature itself. The differentiation of ether into electricity and magnetism is merely a case of sexual differentiation.

As the male is merely the embodiment of the electrical force, so the female is the embodiment of the magnetic force. The feminine spirit, soul, mind, emotion principle, life and body are merely manifestations of the magnetic principle. Femininity is not limited to the form, however, but the seven principles of nature are also magnetic—and, therefore, feminine as well as electric—and, therefore, masculine.

Nature herself is feminine—magnetic—as well as masculine—electric. Male and female, therefore, are merely electricity and magnetism. And the only difference between the male and female is a difference in the rate of vibration.

Man is, therefore, the product of the electric vibration, while woman is the product of the magnetic vibration.

All beings are bisexual. In the male the electrical very much predominates, in the female the magnetic greatly predominates. The sex is determined by the predominating principle. The weaker principle is usually latent, but in the case of the strong-minded woman and the effeminate man, the two principles are much more nearly balanced. Not only is this true, but the personality is in a continuous state of flux. The state of the mind, emotions, soul and spirit becoming for the moment relatively more electrical or magnetic, has the effect of making the principle correspondingly male or female, as the case may be.

The higher principles react upon the physical body, making it in turn more masculine or feminine as the electrical or magnetic principle predominates. In this way the relative balancing of the sexes is continually changing in accordance with the state of the person's life and thought, etc. In this way we can begin to perceive how the superstition of the changing of men into women and women into men originated. Sexual differentiation is, therefore, a matter of differentiation in the rate of vibration.

GOOD AND EVIL.

God and good in the Anglosaxon are synonymous terms. God is the good one, good is the quality of Godlikeness, that is good which brings into closer relation to God. Evil is the reverse. It is that which separates us from God. Because of this original meaning, evil came to mean that which separates and good that which holds together. Good is the principle of union, cohesion, accretion, while evil is the principle of separation, disintegration, dissolution, individuality.

Everything which tends to unite and combine diverse elements is good. Everything which tends to separate, repel and dissolve all combinations, leaving each element independent, is evil. Good is the constructive principle, and evil the destructive principle of nature.

That which unites, constructs and combines the diverse elements is the principle of attraction. All elements attract like elements of opposite polarity. The law of attraction is, therefore, the application of the principle of chemical affinity to the molecules, atoms, etc. It is by reason of the affinity existing between the various atoms and molecules that they mutually attract each other and are bound together and united by adhesion and cohesion, thus forming a structure.

Affinity is the outgrowth of the interaction of the electrical and magnetic forces. Whenever electric and magnetic forces are acting in conjunction, they result in that state of affinity, which produces attraction and, therefore, leads to accretion, union, etc., forming a structure held together by means of its keynote, The harmony of electric and magnetic vibration is, therefore, the essence of good.

It must not be assumed that this applies to the physical plane alone, for, on the contrary, all the planes of nature manifest this same principle. Good on the plane of emotion, the mental plane, the spiritual plane or the plane of the soul is precisely the same in its ultimate essence, as physical good. The point to be fixed in mind is that good of every description and on every plane is merely the harmonious polarizing of the two opposing forces for the production of affinity, leading to the attraction of the diverse elements into union of the same, thus forming a structure on whatever plane of nature it may belong.

Evil is the principle of repulsion operating among the component atoms and molecules of a structure unto the destruction of the keynote, and thus unto the disintegration of the structure and the dissolution of the union existing between the diverse elements composing the same.

Repulsion is due to the absence of affinity,—is due to the

fact that the electrical and magnetic forces are acting in opposition one to another. One neutralizes the other, so that no polarity is possible between the diverse elements. Union is, therefore, impossible,—repulsion resulting in disintegration and dissolution of the entire structure is the result.

Thus the essence of evil is merely the antagonistic activity of the electric and magnetic forces, as good is their harmonious activity. Good is the result of polarity, evil is the absence of polarity. Neither must we suppose this principle of evil to be confined to the physical plane, for on all the planes of nature do we find the manifestations of the principle of antagonism. It is continually tearing down, disintegrating, dissolving and destroying.

Everywhere we go, we see the continuous warfare between the constructive work or good, and the destructive work or evil. The first is ever uniting, the second ever separating. The one ever works for cohesion, the other for disintegration. It is solely a question of polarity or anti-polarity of electro-magnetic energy through harmonious or inharmonious vibration.

STATIONARY AND MOVABLE.

Whenever the molecules constituting a body are revolving round their center of gravity with such a force that they cannot be drawn from their course by any force which may be brought against them, they may be said to be stationary. Not that they do not move, but that they cannot be moved. Their relation cannot be changed by any external force which may be brought to bear upon them. They maintain their regular laws, notwithstanding all outside opposition. This is merely a case of close affinity; the close affinity is due to an intensity of vibration which overpowers all opposing vibration.

When the molecules constituting a body are revolving and

vibrating around their center of gravity with laxity, as to permit an opposing force to drive them out of their course, they may be said to be movable. Their relation may be changed by force from the outside. They are deflected from their regular course with comparative ease. This is merely a case of loose affinity. The loose affinity depends upon a weak state of vibration which may be altered by an opposing vibration.

Also, in another sense, the planetary bodies are movable, in the sense that they have a center of gravity outside of themselves and by reason of the polarity existing between them and this center of gravity, they are moved in accordance with that polarity and the affinity. All bodies containing their center of gravity within themselves are stationary. All bodies having a center of gravity outside and independent of themselves are movable.

The first is, therefore, complete in itself, having both the electric and the magnetic forces equally active and in a state of balance. The second is incomplete, having one pole so weak that it must find the opposite pole outside of itself, and polarize with it in order to attain completion. The only difference between the stationary and the movable is, therefore, a difference in the electro-magnetic polarity growing out of a difference in vibration.

This distinction is not confined to the physical plane alone, but applies to the higher planes of nature as well. The desire elementals, thought forms, Buddhic forms and spirit forms are both stationary and movable, and the law as above outlined, applies to them quite as much as to the physical object.

SQUARE AND OBLONG.

The square is the symbol of perfection. The four sides and the four corners represent the fourfold manifestations of ether, to-wit: positive electricity or oxygen, the element of fire; negative electricity, or hydrogen, the element of water; positive magnetism or carbon, the element of earth; and negative magnetism, or nitrogen, the element of air.

The square, therefore, represents the perfect balance of the positive and negative electric and magnetic forces. It is, therefore, the perfect blending and polarization of the four-fold natural force. Out of this resting place of the fourfold energy proceed all things. The square is, therefore, the complete equilibrium of both the forces and both the poles of the same.

The oblong is a square with something added to extend it in one direction. It is, therefore, not a square, i. e., both the forces are not equally active in both of their poles, but one force or else one pole of each force is stronger than the other, the result being that the activity becomes one sided, giving special activity to the predominating force or pole.

It is this special activity of one principle which is represented by the oblong in contradistinction with the perfect equilibrium of both principles represented by the square. This activity is not confined to physical electricity and magnetism, but extends to all the other principles of nature as well as the physical.

Every activity of thought, emotion and intuition, as well as every activity of the spirit, is a manifestation of one of these states of electro-magnetic activity, either the perfect square or the oblong.

WET AND DRY.

Substances become wet because of the presence of moisture in them. They are dried out by the action of heat. Heat is caused by raising of the molecular vibration. Therefore, when we raise the rate of vibration of the molecules until it reaches a certain point of intensity, moisture disappears, the substance becomes dry; the higher the rate of vibration the dryer the substance becomes until it reaches the melting point. Dryness is also a characteristic of electricity, while moisture is a characteristic of magnetism. Therefore, a substance becomes dry in proportion as it passes from the magnetic to the electric stage. When it has reached the electric vibration, the higher it becomes, the more of the magnetic is eliminated, and thus the dryer it becomes.

On the other hand, as the magnetic vibration predominates, the substance becomes moist, and the more extremely magnetic it becomes, the more moist it becomes. Anything is, therefore, moist in proportion as it is magnetic, and dry in proportion as it is electric. Not only is this the case on the physical plane, but also on all the other planes of nature. Vital electricity is dry, and vital magnetism wet. Mental electricity is dry, and mental magnetism wet. Psychical or Buddhic electricity is dry and psychic or Buddhic magnetism is wet. Spiritual magnetism is wet, and spiritual electricity is dry.

Again, the two poles of both electricity and magnetism are diverse; positive electricity is much dryer than the negative, and negative magnetism is not so wet as the positive. It may be readily seen from the foregoing that the quality of dryness is merely the electrical quality in anything, and the quality of moisture is merely the magnetic quality. The only difference, therefore, between the wetness and dryness is a difference in electro-magnetic polarity.

From the foregoing remarks on the pairs of opposites, it may be seen that we have a means of reaching the conception of things in themselves. We may comprehend the abstract and not merely the concrete,—the noumenon and not merely the phenomena. We may comprehend right and left in the abstract without relating them to anything, may conceive of them in terms of the absolute. Likewise evenness and oddness may be conceived in the abstract without thinking of any concrete thing to be either even or odd. In the same way we can conceive of the abstract principles of heat and cold without thinking of any concrete object to be either hot or cold. Also, we may conceive of the abstract principle of hardness and softness without thinking of anything being either hard or soft. Abstract light and abstract darkness may be in the same way conceived separate and apart from all consciousness of any material object to be affected by the light or the darkness. Likewise, also may we conceive of the abstract principle of masculinity and femininity separate and apart from any concrete thing to be either male or female. Also the abstract principle of good and evil may be comprehended separate and apart from anything to be either good or evil. Likewise the conception of abstract mobility and immobility separate and apart from anything to be moved or to remain stationary, becomes possible. Also we may conceive of the abstract quality of squareness and oblongness as things in themselves, separate and apart from any concrete object to be either square or oblong. And we may also conceive of the abstract principles of wetness and dryness as things in themselves, separate and apart from any concrete object to be either wet or dry.

Let the student try to realize that these opposite qualities are all things in themselves, are all abstract principles and not dependent upon any concrete object for their existence but are self-existent so far as the concrete world is concerned. And that the concrete objects which show forth these qualities are merely the vehicles through which these abstract principles are being manifested to our outward senses, but that the abstract principles are in no way to depend upon such concrete objects for their activity. Let him further conceive of them as merely the activities of the electrical and magnetic principles of nature, acting on her various planes.

When he understands this, let him conceive electricity and magnetism themselves as merely the twofold manifestation of the one principle pertaining to that particular plane of nature. Lastly, let him conceive of this manifestation as merely the effect of the two states of the vibratory action of the one principle.

When all this is perfectly plain to him, so that he understands that all things are merely matters of magneto-electric activity, and that electro-magnetism is merely the twofold activity of the one principle, and lastly that the twofold manifestation is the result of a different rate of vibration, hence the whole thing is merely a matter of vibration, and that this law not only applies to the physical world, but to everything else on whatever plane; when all this is clearly seen and comprehended, by the student, he has solved the law of opposites.

LESSON III.

The Law of Balance.

The law of compensation rules throughout nature. It is an utter impossibility for force to be expended in one direction without being drawn from another. The negative and the positive are everywhere present in manifestations. There can be no good without evil; no gain without loss; nothing can be received without giving; everything must be paid for.

The statement of Jesus "Cast your bread upon the waters and it will return to you after many days", is an absolute scientific truth. You can never give up anything, can never sacrifice anything without the law bringing the compensation. On the other hand, you can never acquire anything without the law requiring you to give up something in return. The law of renunciation is the very secret of all acquisition. Success can only be accomplished through sacrifice.

The idea that so many people have, that we can develop on all planes and on all lines—financially, materially, physically, spiritually, intellectually, etc., and reach the highest on all those lines, is absolutely untrue. Man's spiritual progress is in direct ratio to his abandoning or renouncing the material, the physical. The same may be said of his intellectual progress.

New-thoughters are quite in the habit of making the statement, "my own will come to me", and this is perfectly correct. Your own will always come to you, but your own is not that which you desire, but that which you embody, that which has become a part of your nature, of your very being. Therefore, in order to bring anything to you, you must first

30

develop the counterpart of it within yourself. In a word, it is only as we polarize with a force or principle in nature that we are able to draw it to us.

The positive seeks the negative; therefore, by simply sitting and desiring your own to come to you, you get nothing because you haven't anything to begin with. You may sit, hold your hands and expect your own to come to you, and it will come, because you have developed nothing within yourself; therefore, your own is nothing. Consequently, the only way to acquire, to demonstrate anything is by first developing the corresponding state within your own being.

What we desire, that which becomes a dominant desire of our being, regulates and directs the activity of our principles. Evolution is by use all through life. It is by giving exercise to certain faculties, powers, attributes of the being that they are developed. During the time when the desire is centered upon material things, the being is completely insulated from the spiritual and of everything else, while, on the other hand, when the mind is centered upon the desire for acquiring the spiritual or intellectual, it is insulated to the physical, the material, the commercial. Consequently, so long as one is trying to demonstrate financial success, it is an utter impossibility for him to demonstrate spiritual, moral or intellectual success.

It has been observed from time immemorial that a great knowledge of the truth, a deep insight into nature, a high spiritual character, are never found in conjunction with a successful financial career. The apparent exceptions to this rule are found in the cases of those persons who have acquired their wealth by inheritance or in some accidental manner. The person who, by his own efforts, acquires wealth, cannot by the nature of things, acquire anything higher. This is the reason why mystics find it necessary to abandon business, commerce, the worldly life, in fact, all personal ambition, and in many instances, take the vow of perpetual poverty in order that they may develop spiritual knowledge and power.

As long as the attention is concentrated upon the acquisition of wealth or anything of that character, anything of a physical nature, it is utterly impossible for it to come in touch with the higher realms, the higher planes of nature and, therefore, get that spiritual force which will result in the spiritual development of the being. Likewise, selfishness of this character will prevent the acquisition of truth. The business man attaches a commercial value to all things.

Truth for truth's sake, has to him, absolutely no value. Because of this fact we see that among these New-thoughters and other modern philosophers who are holding to this idea of demonstrating success, these practical people who are always thinking of the commercial utility, the value from the standpoint of success of those things, pragmatism has become the dominant philosophical tendency. Pragmatism does not ask, is a thing true, but is it practical; will it work? What can I do with it in my business? The pragmatic philosopher cares nothing for truth. He only cares for the utilitarian value of truth, and if he can use a lie as successfully as he can the truth, the one is equally valuable with the other.

This tendency absolutely insulates the mind from the reception of truth, for the law governing the mental plane is such that in order to come in tune, in order to polarize with that plane and thus come into touch with the truth in its highest sense, it is absolutely necessary to be devoted without question, without any reserve whatever, to truth, for its own sake and not because of any personal utility which may be found therein. The only way by which truth may be attained is by an absolutely unselfish, disinterested attachment to it. If we aspire to use truth, we can never find it. Truth is a jealous mistress; she will not consent to be the tool of her lover, but must be met on her own plane and sought for her own sake.

Therefore we can never arrive at an understanding of the truth except by giving up, abandoning, renouncing things of a material nature to an extent, and on the other hand, we cannot renounce, lose our interest in those things without, as a result, the mind being withdrawn from the material and turned to the higher things, and thus we attain to higher development and a realization of that which we seek.

As long as the consciousness is centered in the self; as long as man thinks of all things in reference to how they affect him, he shuts himself off from the universe which is governed by the spirit of the high, not that of the individual, and as a result absolute knowledge, cosmic consciousness, becomes an utter impossibility. Because of this fact, the adherent of the New Thought movement with its ultra-egocentric character, cannot possibly come into tune with the universe and acquire an understanding of absolute truth; neither can he attain spiritual development, because of the fact that he cuts himself loose from the great universal Whole, and it is only by polarizing with this cosmic whole, that man is able to understand it.

Only by identifying yourself with nature are you able to understand nature. Therefore we can readily see that nothing is ever lost, but on the contrary, whatever we send forth is bound to return again sooner or later, because in giving, we do not give away, but we make a deposit to nature. In the bank of nature we are making a deposit, which will be paid sooner or later, not in the same coin which is deposited, but in a better; therefore, the more we give, the more we receive. By giving we become the creditor of the universe.

On the other hand, anything which we receive must be paid for in the same way; not in the coin which we have received, but in some other. By receiving, we become the debtor of nature, and must pay the debt. This is why Jesus says, "It is more blessed to give than to receive", because by giving, we are placing nature under obligations to us, and nature always fulfills her obligations; by receiving something which has not been earned, we are placing ourselves under obligations to nature, and she demands that all obligations shall be fulfilled.

Sacrifice is, therefore, the very door to affluence. It is by giving that we receive. Self-sacrifice is, therefore, not a duty, but the best possible business policy. As we renounce all desire of material things, our attention is removed from them. Having become positive to the material things, we, as a result, become negative to spiritual and intellectual things, and consequently attract them to us. For this reason the law of renunciation and self-sacrifice is the road to understanding, spirituality and emancipation. The person who really deserves anything is bound to receive it merely because of deserving it; and the person who secures anything without having deserved it, will find that the acquisition of the same has been a distinct disadvantage to him, shutting him off effectively from all progress after higher things.

We can see, therefore, that the way to progress is to do your work, do all that is in your power, asking for nothing in return, and by this holding disinterested action, the service will open the way for an unlimited influx from without. If we expect any compensation whatever for what we do, we limit the degree of our self sacrifice, and in proportion as our renunciation is limited, so will the compensation which the law brings to us, be limited likewise.

Man is, therefore, benefitting himself in exact proportion as he benefits others; likewise he is injuring himself in exact proportion as he injures others. He cannot possibly do any good without receiving back the return. Neither can he in any manner do an evil or injury without being paid in return for it. For this reason we are best serving our own interests when we are serving those of others. We are doing the greatest injury to ourselves when we are injuring another.

Egoism and altruism are, therefore, identical. The man who is intelligently selfish is the most altruistic, because he realizes that by being altruistic he is conferring the greatest benefit upon himself. If men would only realize this law, they would see that they could not afford to injure another because they would by so doing, injure themselves. They would not hesitate to do any manner of good because they would realize by so doing that they would simply receive back good in return. All is justice, nothing is lost, no deed or thought or word, either good or bad, can be expressed without bringing its return to the expresser.

We often hear persons talking about a successful life, or the man who has succeeded. A very interesting question would be what constitutes success. The average person measures the successful life in proportion to the amount of money, or at least of physical comforts which the person has secured. You realize that the acquisition of knowledge and spiritual attainment are measures of the greatest success. You will see a person whose knowledge or spiritual attainment is the envy of these so-called successful people, and yet he is what they call a failure, but it was only by being a failure in material things that he became a success in the intellectual or spiritual. Intellectual and spiritual success is only attainable through material failure. Material success is only attainable through intellectual and spiritual failure.

Those who believe in demonstrating what they call success, have spoken of parties after this wise: Oh, that person has the knowledge, he understands the law thoroughly, and I would give anything in the world if I had the understanding that that person possesses; there is only one thing about him that I can't understand and that is why a person of his knowledge and understanding should be poor. He ought to be rich with the knowledge that he has. To whom it might be said, that it was because the person was poor, and did not waste any of his valuable time making money, that he was able to acquire this knowledge. The reason why he is so far superior in the line of understanding above these successful people, is because he has never striven for what they call success. His whole mind, his whole power, in fact, has been concentrated upon the acquisition of knowledge. Because he renounced the desire for material things, he opened the way by which he may acquire the intellectual and the spiritual.

Others have been known to say, I cannot understand how it is that with your great knowledge, your wonderful understanding of the truth, for you understand the law governing the psychical and occult realms far better than any man I ever saw, how it is that you are not able to demonstrate success. Now, let us see, if a man acquires the most accurate knowledge of those realms of any person living, or even if he falls far short of that accomplishment, but has a profound knowledge of nature, has he not been successful in his struggle for the acquisition of those things?

The successful man is the man who succeeds in accomplishing his purpose. If a man succeeds in learning a law of nature, is not he just as successful as the man who succeeds in making a fortune? It is all a matter of the standard by which we measure success. Persons who have different ideals will naturally consider success to be represented by different achievements, but the successful man is the man who realizes his ideal, whatever it may be, and no one else is successful.

What is it which causes one man to realize his ideal, while another fails in doing so? The answer is quite simple. The one succeeds who renounces every other desire, every other aspiration when it comes to comparing with his ideal. The one purpose of his existence is the realization of the ideal and because of this fact he becomes the very embodiment of this purpose, this ideal: he becomes wholly negative to it, and positive to everything which will conflict with it. As a result, he is absolutely certain to succeed; whereas the man whose efforts are divided, whose forces are diffused, who does not put his whole soul into the struggle, is bound to fail.

When the man realizes that material things are not worth having, but the only thing of value is the spiritual, or at least, the mental understanding of the truth, he naturally puts forth all his efforts to acquire that which he regards as most valuable. As a result, he realizes that. He demonstrates success even if he starves to death, because he has succeeded in realizing his ideal. The man who does not realize his ideal is a total failure, no matter if he owns the earth.

It must be borne in mind that this law of balance is not merely a moral principle; it is not to be conceived in the sense of a reward, a man's good intentions or anything of the kind, but it is simply the application of the law of polarity. It is a simple problem of chemical affinity. We separate from the lower and unite with the higher; we unite with the lower, we must necessarily be separated from the higher.

It is true there may be a symmetrical development all along the line, but a person who is proficient in all lines can excel in none. The specialist is at all times far superior to the general practitioner. Likewise, the person who renounces one line of effort in achievement in order that he may devote all his attention to the other, is bound to far outstrip the one who tries to work on all lines. This is the law. There is no escape from it. As man sows, so will he reap. He can never reap that which he has not sown. Thus it must always be borne in mind that this law is as fundamental a law of nature as anything can be. It is a form of chemical affinity and, therefore, cannot be defeated.

We escape from evil by doing good. This law is, in reality, the secret underlying all ethical systems. When man intelligently awakens to a realization of the Law of Balance, he will in that way alone, attain unto the most perfect conception of right relations, because he will know that he must pay for what he gets, and must get what he pays for. The solution of good and evil, right and wrong, and everything of the kind, is, therefore, contained in an understanding of this law.

Those silly idealists or fanatics, who have renounced everything of a worldly character, have given up themselves entirely to the contemplation of the ideal, have, therefore, been far more practical, shown far more common sense and business judgment than anything else. They have realized that there was a certain end which they wished to accomplish, and have known that the only way by which they might accomplish this end is by giving up, withdrawing their effort from everything which would withdraw them from this activity.

There are two kinds of riches: Those without and those within. The stoics were right in realizing and maintaining that to have the mind centered upon the acquisition of external riches, would prevent the acquisition of internal riches. As long as the fallacy of owning things continues to actuate a person, it is utterly impossible for him to be anything. The wealth of the soul is never compatible with the desire for external wealth. Man must decide whether he wants to have something or to be something. The two do not go together. The cynics, therefore, in teaching that man is rich in proportion to the things which he could do without, not in proportion to the things which he had, were perfectly correct. The purpose of philosophy was to make the soul independent of the appearance of their finding within itself full satisfaction for all its aspirations asking nothing but that it might be great; and when we realize this lesson, we cease to worry about the compensation which we are to receive for our superior attainments, for we realize that the possession of those superior attainments is far superior to any other compensation which we might possibly receive.

Indifference to the appearance of things, opens the way to the attainment of reality. The man who has no fear of the external, is the only one who is free. All others are slaves. The man attains this state of not fearing the external because he realizes that the external cannot give him anything worth having, neither can it deprive him of anything of value. He is, therefore, absolutely independent, because he is absolutely indifferent to either the friendship or enmity of anything, outside of himself.

He says to the universe, I need you not. Having become thus independent of everything and everybody outside of himself, he is ready to serve in an absolutely disinterested manner, doing good without hope, expectation or desire of any reward, for the simple reason that there is nothing that can be given him that he wants.

As long as man works and co-operates with the idea of mutual helpfulness, mutual assistance, service for service, his good deeds are selfish. Therefore, their fruit must be limited, but when he renounces all desire for anything from another, all expectation or wish for help, gratitude or anything in return, acting purely from principle, he thus removes all limitations from his service. He serves in the same disinterested manner that God does. Therefore, he opens the way for an unlimited return.

The person who completely casts out all desire for anything in the way of return for his services, immediately opens the way for the greatest possible return. It is the law of balance, bringing back to you whatever you put in. This is the secret to attainment. No one can ever attain the heights except as he follows along this path.

The man who has separated himself from all selfish or personal considerations, who does not ask for gratitude or love, immediately opens the way by which he may enter into that unity with the Divine, for he has acquired divine attributes. As God shows no partiality and expects no return but causes the sun to shine upon the evil and the good, sends rain upon the just and the unjust, acting from the standpoint of principle absolutely, so man, by expressing those qualities, separates himself from all mundane attractions, cuts himself loose from humanity by extinguishing human frailties, and unites himself with God by expressing Divine attributes.

In just that proportion that you put into practice this general principle of renunciation of the external, so will you acquire the internal. In just that proportion that you cease to desire the lower will you receive the higher. The positive must respond to the negative all the way through life.

People are all the time kicking because their prayers are not always answered. Prayers are always answered.

Prayer is the sincere desire of the heart, and that which is sincerely desired, will be drawn to the being who desires it. Men are always asking for material things, and then kick because they do not acquire the spiritual. Man is hoping, praying, working and striving to get things of the external, and then is worried because of his internal poverty. He is so anxious to get something that he never has time to be anything. Character, internal worth, soul growth, are only possible when the desire and aspiration are fixed upon those qualities. So long as we desire that which is without, we will absolutely be unable to develop anything within. Nothing can keep you out of your own, and if you make the material your own, you will get it, and if you make the spiritual your own, you will get that, but you have got to pay for whatever you receive.

Spiritual wealth is paid for by material poverty, and material wealth is paid for by spiritual poverty. Spiritual poverty brings material wealth. Material poverty tends in many instances to bring spiritual wealth. It is altogether a question of the direction in which the mind and heart are concentrated. Where a man's treasure is, there will his heart be also; likewise, where a man's heart is, there will his treasure be pretty apt to develop itself.

The Law of Balance gives the key to the demonstration of success in any line which man may aspire to succeed in. The law is perfect, and cannot fail. Beggars are failures in the spiritual and mental world, usually as much as in the physical. The man who is not willing to pay for what he receives from nature, is just as much of a bum as the man who is not willing to pay for his bread upon the physical plane, and bums never succeed in the development of character. The Law of Balance must be recognized and obeyed. Being recognized and obeyed, it will lead the soul to the highest possible attainment.

LESSON IV.

The Law of Rhythm.

The apparently contradicting principles and operations and forces of nature are in reality but positive and negative aspects of the same thing. The duality which we find throughout all nature is merely a manifestation of unity. It is only in this way, by realizing the paradoxical character of all things, that we are able to arrive at absolute truth. Short of this we can only deal in the relative. We speak of things under certain qualifications, but we only conceive of them in relation to something else.

In order to establish an absolute code of ethics, we must understand the law of rhythm in regard to all things in the universe. Take, for instance, those ethical principles, such as right and wrong; what do they mean? Originally right meant straight, and wrong meant crooked. In order to reach an absolute standard of right and wrong it is necessary to recognize the twofold relation of all things and to get a view of that in relation to which things or actions are straight or crooked. When we realize that matter is merely a manifestation of spirit; that nature is an emanation and manifestation of God, manifested with more or less perfection, then realizing this, and also the fact that all things in the universe are now in manifestation on a lower plane, have gone from, as it were, and are on the way to return to God; that man is a manifestation of God, and is here for the purpose of returning to God. Realizing this, we then have a criterion by which we may measure the rightness or wrongness of any given

42

action. All actions are right in proportion as their tendency is to lead the actor directly into union with God. They are wrong in exact proportion as their tendency is to cause the actor to deviate from that direct path which would cause man to be brought to God. It will be seen, therefore, that only is right which tends to union with God; that only is wrong which tends to prevent that union, which leads aside from the path which will lead to union with God.

True ethics are, therefore, theocentric and not anthropocentric, all actions being right or wrong as they relate man to God. Every man must, therefore, have a code of ethics, to a certain extent at least, of his own, because that which would bring one person to God may be different from that course which would lead another to God. If a given action has a tendency to bring the actor in direct touch with God, that action is absolutely right for him, while it might have the effect of preventing another person from reaching that state. If so, it would be wrong for him.

Take now the question of good and evil: Good properly means God. Evil, occultly, means that which separates. Used in contradistinction to good, it means that which separates from God, that which draws away from Him, carries the person away from God. Good, used in opposition to evil, would, then, be that which tended to union with God. The whole mystery of good and evil is, therefore, summed up in the bringing to God, or separation from Him. This is the only conception of good and evil which presents them in their actualities.

Now take the question of good and bad: good, being equivalent to God, means that which is Godlike in character. Bad, as the reverse, is that which is anti-Godlike in its character. We can, therefore, see that the only question involved in any absolute ethical proposition, is this: Does it tend to union with God, or, on the other hand, to separation from

God? In one sense of the word, good also represents the principle of accretion throughout all nature, human or otherwise, and evil, the principle of separation—disintegration. We may say, then, that good is union, evil is separation.

All manifestations are first accomplished through separation, and then through union. In a word, antagonism is the means by which manifestation is accomplished. Were there no evil,—separation—there would be no good—union. Everything passes out from God during the process of individualization. After a time the return begins. When this individuality, having been developed, is lost, union is the result. Thus all development is cyclical. There is first a downward sweep into matter; then a home-stretch out of matter into spirit. Progress is the outgrowth of this twofold operation. Without the descent, the ascent is an impossibility. Without involution there can be no evolution. As we descend into matter, that is pass away from God, we first learn to appreciate the value of God. We very often hear the question asked, why does God permit evil? For the simple reason that without this antagonism, this opposition, it is impossible for any manifestation to take place. Before man is able to appreciate the value of service to God, of harmony, of union, he must have first fully realized the terrible consequences of separation, individualization, evil. Until man has tried separation, he does not realize the value of union. This principle is very nicely expressed in the parable of the prodigal son. Here we have a young man leaving his father's house, demanding his part of the estate, going forth to develop his ego, to express his individuality. As long as the money lasts, that is, as long as he is able to enjoy this attitude, this life of separation, he thinks nothing of his father's house. At last they find him starving, feeding swine, reduced to the lowest depth of degradation, fully realizing the terrible consequences of the past life. Finally, having been reduced down to this lowest point—having, in a word, developed his individuality, he realizes the total uselessness of it. Realizing how perfectly unfruitful is this kind of a life, at last he says, "I will rise and go unto my father," realizing the position of a servant is better, altogether more desirable than that of a freeman. His individuality is now surrendered; he has laid it down and he starts on the return to his father's house; here we find him coming back. He is now received. His father does not chase after him; he does not send missionaries after him; he makes absolutely no effort to bring him back. He allows him to go ahead, do as he pleases, expressing his individuality until such time as he fully realizes the worthlessness of this thing, and prefers the position of a servant to this individuality. Even so, the soul when it wanders from home, going into the path of evil, going away from God, is expressing its individuality. God makes no effort to reclaim it, because He knows that it must have this experience; it must find out in the bitter school of experience that individuality is most undesirable. Realizing this, He allows it to go ahead in its own way. It is not interrupted; it is permitted to travel the path of evil until it has learned that individuality is worthless. Then it is ready to begin the return, to come back into union with God.

This spirit of antagonism is, therefore, the very means of offering an opportunity for the highest development of the good.

We have very often heard the question, "If God is all powerful, why doesn't He kill the Devil?" For the simple reason that the devil is of too much value at the present stage of the game. He cannot be spared. It is because of this continual war between good and evil that the highest attainment—or, for that matter, any attainment at all, is possible. Were there no darkness, there would be no light. Were there no cold, there would be no heat. In like manner,

were there no evil, there would be no good. Were there
nothing wrong, there would be nothing right.

The whole foundation of all these classifications merely
consists in a relative differentiation. This relative differentiation is made in respect to some principle of which the two are
aspects.

The law of rhythm is mastered when we realize that the
various opposites are merely the twofold aspect of unity. By
realizing this, we polarize them, making one the positive and
the other the negative pole of this unity. The result is that
harmony is brought out of contradiction, order out of chaos,
agreement out of contradiction. The person having realized
the law of rhythm is in a position then to intelligently condemn no one, realizing that everything has its place; nothing
is useless; the evil is just as necessary as the good at certain
stages of evolution. It is in this sense that the aphorism
"always good" is found to be true. Always good, because the
evil is preparing the way for the manifestation of the good. It
is because of this law of rhythm that all occult teachers teach
in paradoxes, the paradox being the only way by which a
complete truth may be presented. This is the reason why
there are always two sides to every question. One aspect
presents the positive, the other the negative pole of the principle involved; consequehtly we must teach in paradoxes in
order that by contradiction, we may present both sides of the
question. Thus this law of polarity or rhythm, gives us a
glimpse of absolute truth.

The law of non-resistance is a natural outgrowth of the
recognition of the law of rhythm, and why? For the simple
reason that a person recognizing the law or rhythm, sees that
all evil is good in its ultimate tendencies, because this experience is necessary in a certain stage of human development. Now, because the sinner is in the very act of sinning,
doing what is for him, necessary, in order that he may learn

his lesson, we should not resist his having this experience, because depriving him of the experience will mean to prevent his finding God, as he can only apprehend the value of Divine services by living in rebellion against God.

What is sin, in reality? Sin is a transgression of law. Law, in this sense, is the statement or presentation of the divine will. Sin, therefore, is merely the result of the human will arrayed in opposition to the divine will. Righteousness, used in contradistinction to sin, is merely a human will being governed and subordinated to the Divine will and acting consistently with this state or condition.

The difference, then, between a sinner and a righteous person is merely the difference between a person exercising a free will and one whose will is subordinated to the divine will; and in plain words, this is merely the difference between an individualist and a servant of God. Man, by continual transgression—that is to say, continual transgression and rebellion against the will of God, ultimately learns the very important lesson that subordination to that will is much better for him than individual independence of will. He quits sinning because he sees that it is not good for him, that it is not proper so to do; in other words, he surrenders himself to divine guidance. Sin, therefore, is permitted as a part of the racial experience. It is by going through this ordeal, that character is developed; consequently sin is just as necessary in the present stage of our evolution as righteousness. Because we know this, therefore we do not condemn the actions of another. We know that he is merely getting his schooling. We may say he is undeveloped, young, so to speak, in the process of childhood, but still he is not depraved, he is simply learning a very important lesson. It is in this sense that the saying is true, "to know all, is to forgive all", because knowing, understanding the relation between all activities, we know that those evil tendencies are just as important as the good, in working out this transformation and development of character.

We can now understand the purpose of the apparent injustice, inequality, misery, suffering and privations which are seen all around us. They are but the environment which makes development possible. They stimulate sin and evil by drifting along in accordance with their suggestions; man develops the evil, learns the consequence of transgression—something that he could not possibly learn otherwise. By resisting those tendencies and developing in spite of their influence the opposite, he thus forms the good character which brings him nearer and nearer to God. Thus this hostile environment to virtue is merely the gymnasium in which the moral athlete develps his ethical muscles.

Evil is, therefore, an important instrument in the hands of God for the perfecting of a character. Nothing can manifest except through opposition. It is from the law of opposites, as reduced to rhythm, that the most perfect application of all the activities of nature become possible. It is through it that the value of obedience is learned.

What should then be the attitude of the Master of this law in regard to the evil which we see around us? All social evils are due to one, and only one cause: Humanity is traveling the evil path; it is not living in harmony with God, nor even trying to do so. Our social evils are, therefore, the legitimate outgrowth of a humanity traveling the path of separation. We should not, therefore, attempt to remove them. They are just what we want. The man who refuses to subordinte his will to the Divine, but insists upon exercising his individuality, upon developing his ego, is merely getting what is coming to him, when the evils of society overtake him. Not only is this true but those evils are the very force that sooner or later will teach him the futility and the unfruitfulness of any effort to live independent of God. The man who would rather be free than to be God's servant, is a fool, and the sooner he finds it out, the better it is for him, and the natural, inevitable consequences of this freedom are the best means of teaching him the lesson; therefore, we should make no effort to save him from this most salutary experience. Not only is this true, but the person understanding the law, need not expect to reform or lift up the person who is trying to be free, to be an individual, to develop an ego. Let him go ahead his own way. He cannot receive the truth until he is ready for it. It is only when he has finished his course that he will be ready for the return path; therefore, do not evangelize, do not proselyte. If you see one who is ready, who is searching for the Divine will, really wants to reform—wants to conform to it and is asking what it is, then help him to return, but the man who does not want to return should be left alone. As long as man's nature, taste, tendencies, are evil, let him go ahead and enjoy the evil to the limit. Only when he searches for the good, can the good be imparted to him. It is utterly useless. Take a swine and wash him, dress him up, turn him loose and he will seek a mud puddle just the same. If the human swine wish to lie in the mud, let them do so by all means. Do not waste any valuable energy trying to teach them a better way of life. As long as they enjoy the mud, let them wallow in it. It is their nature and so let them give expression to this nature. When they get tired of mud and desire something better, then help them to get it, but do not waste any effort trying to make people something that they do not wish to be. This is the secret which the law of rhythm has to impart to us. The low, degraded, debased light is just as necessary at certain stages of human culture as the highest, most aesthetic, more spiritual; therefore, it is not for you to interfere with those persons who are traveling the downward path. It is for them; they must express and develop that phase of life activity. Those who realize the worthlessness and baseness of that phase of life, and as a result, are trying to live on the higher plane, you may help. Bear in mind it is only those who have started on the return path who can be helped upward. While man is exercising and developing the evil, there is absolutely nothing which can be done that will change his course. He must reach the bottom before he begins to return toward the top. The individuality must be developed before it can be surrendered. Had man remained in harmony with God, all the time, he would have possessed no character; his mentality would not have been developed; he would be just as his creator made him without having established any definite character. It was thus by starting on the path of evil, or separation, that he was able to develop character. When this character has been fully developed, he will thus have secured a more perfect degree of knowledge, understanding and character with which he may serve God than he could possibly have possessed without such experience. The individualist is, therefore, necessary for this purpose, as a realization of the purpose of God, just as much so as the one who has attained cosmic consciousness. The person who has renounced his individuality is merely on his return, traveling toward God, while the one expressing his individuality is traveling away from God. Both are necessary to express human progress. The race will derive the benefit accrued from the actions of both.

We are, therefore, able to appreciate the relations which all actions have to the purpose of life, namely: Union with God. All actions derive their character from their relation to this point. The person who realizes the law of rhythm, therefore, is perfectly satisfied with everything in the universe. He is just as well satisfied with the evil as he is with the good, knowing that out of the apparent contradictions seen in the world, unity, good and harmony must grow. For this reason he is content, satisfied with everything as he sees it, knowing that it is all merely a question of positive or negative polarity.

The question may be asked, what relation has this to motion and number? Merely this; that God has a certain rhythm, and that mental activity which is the spring from which actions flow, is or is not vibrating to this rhythm. If man is acting in harmony with the will of God, then his own vibration approaches the Divine Rhythm. If, on the contrary, he is traveling the path of evil, and, therefore, is acting in opposition to the Divine will, his thought produces a rhythm decidedly different and decidedly antagonistic to the Divine rhythm.

It is for this reason that we speak of harmony as being a stillness, as action having ceased, because the rhythm in man as separate and apart from God, which will give rise to all those activities, has now ceased. The only rhythm which is operative is that of the Divine. Man's own rhythm has ceased. As man, he moves and vibrates no longer, for this reason: the whole problem of good is merely a matter of setting up within man the Divine vibration in opposition to his own human or individualized vibration; consequently this whole problem of good and evil is a question of vibration, a question of motion, of number or rhythm. When the proper rhythm is established, the individual rhythm disappears. When this is done, the individual disappears—is merged in God.

The mystery of evil is, therefore, solved through the law of rhythm. The person in possession of this law, has the key which harmonizes all of the apparent contradictions in the universe. This is, therefore, the true secret of Mastership. Without this knowledge the universe is like a shoreless sea; we know not whither we go, nor from whence we came. We do not know the meaning of it all, but when once put into possession of this master-key, we are able to see harmony in apparent discord; order in apparent chaos, peace amid these antagonisms, and we can say, "It is the work of God, and He doeth all things well." The man who can see the end from the beginning, knows that the harmony is complete. He sees the system in operation throughout all things. It is only to the limited vision which can see only two or three points, that apparent discord appears. There is nothing wrong in the ultimate.

We are going through a process of development, and out of all this discord and disharmony, perfection must come; therefore, the person knowing the law of rhythm is willing to wait, with the ultimate realization of the purpose of life, knowing what it is, being able to trace the terminate purpose which is operating throughout all this confusion and slowly but surely, reducing it to harmony.

LESSON V.

The Music of the Spheres.

In ancient Greece there appeared a character who, as a philosopher, was unmistakably the greatest Greece ever produced; one of the greatest philosophers that the world has ever produced; not only a philosopher, but a scientist, an artist, a mystic, one of whom the world was not worthy and has never been worthy of since; one who, notwithstanding his greatness, notwithstanding the fact that geometry has ever since employed his theorems and found them superior to those of any other geometrician; one whose mathematics and whose mathematical propositions proved absolutely beyond improvement, whose astronomical teachings have been adopted, and who died more than five centuries before Christ, who founded the very same system of astronomy that we now teach, namely, the Copernican system—the character who as a musician, discovered some of the greatest principles known to music—the inventor of the musical scale, and the one who discovered the fact that the length of a musical string determines the numerical value of the note and chord. We know that he discovered this, becaue he invented a musical instrument by the moving of pressure at a certain distance, by which different notes could be struck on that same string, thereby playing a number of strains by moving the pressure at a certain distance that various chords might be struck. And yet, notwithstanding the fact that, standing practically alone, this man accomplished these things which science has been compelled to recognize, he has been branded as a charlatan, as a mountebank and an ignoramus. Indeed, the scientific gentlemen have seen fit to denominate this character the greatest mathematician and geometrician known to the ancient world, and at the same time an impotent charlatan. This ancient light, Pythagoras, was the founder of the Pythagorean school of philosophy, probably the greatest man known in the history of philosophy. Pythagoras would have been a wonderful character quite acceptable to our scientific gentlemen, had he confined himself to the physical, had he only dealt in those things which were in accordance with the physical ideas of our modern teachers, but there were two or three mistakes which Pythagoras made, if he intended to stand well with modern thought. In the first place, he did not scatter broadcast his doctrines; he taught the principal points of his science and philosophy in secret and taught them to initiates only, and then he taught what he knew. He was not such a fool, after all, because Socrates was compelled to drink hemlock quite a number of years afterwards for teaching these things publicly. Pythagoras had sense enough to keep it private and teach it to his disciples only. In lecturing to his pupils, he concealed himself so he could not be seen, and at night he wore a robe and dressed himself in such a way that when they saw him at night, it inspired them with awe, and for a number of these reasons he was not liked very well. Then another thing; Pythagoras was in possession of a very high psychological development; he saw a lot of things that other people could not see and heard a lot of things that other people could not hear, and he was crazy enough to tell the people these things and put them in possession of the facts which they could not find out for themselves. So, strange to say, Pythagoras is denounced for keeping back the truth from the public, and in the next breath, for telling them things that they could not find out for themselves.

The greatest offense which Pythagoras committed was in talking about the Music of the Spheres. He told his disciples that the spheres themselves in their activities, produced music, the planetary revolutions and all the activities of the heavenly bodies were producing music; that this was not simply discordant sound, but it was real music, and that the universe was ruled by music, and that musical harmony was the creating and controlling principle throughout the universe. Had he stopped at this and merely philosophized, they might have claimed that he was a crank, but unfortunately in those days of materialistic guesswork, Pythagoras claimed that he had heard this Music of the Spheres himself and that he had audible evidence in regard to the matter and, therefore, he, of course was a liar. Why, nobody else had heard it; therefore, Pythagoras lied. Any person who hears or sees something that other people do not hear or see is a liar. We believe in democracy, we scientific folks, and we cannot afford to have anyone superior to us. We have got to do this in order to preserve the infallibility of science, and so Pythagoras lied.

But Pythagoras did not lie. The Music of the Spheres is a fact. He was not the only one who heard it. He was the only one who talked about hearing it very much, because the balance of us have learned better, by the treatment that Pythagoras received—that is all. We do not say very much about it, but we, ourselves, have heard it thousands of times, and there are beings in the world who have heard the Music of the Spheres, there are clairvoyants who have even seen it, for music can be seen as well as heard, if you have the eyes with which to see it.

Let us see if we can get at the foundation of this and approach it philosophically and try and establish the fact of the music of the spheres on a scientific and philosophical basis.

Everything in the universe is the product of motion. Inertia is not. We used to be taught in philosophy that inertia was a fundamental principle of matter and that matter was always inert unless motion was imparted to it, but that is not true. There is not any such thing as inertia, and if an atom were ever for one second to stop, the universe would be torn to pieces. Just one atom would wreck the universe if it could actually stop. There is no such thing as inertia, but everywhere is motion—vibration, or motion and number, as Pythagoras called it. In all the planes of nature we see this vibratory activity going on. What are we to conclude? Color, sound and form are inseparably connected with all vibratory activity. Whenever the smallest atoms are vibrating to a certain rhythm, as a result they are drawn together and assume a definite geometrical figure, and as a result they also produce a definite sound and at the same time a definite color, shade or tint, as the case may be, and so the universe is capable of infinite gradations in this line of color, sound and form.

When the particles or atoms—we might say, or spirit, Nirvana—are drawn together by a certain rate of vibration, the result is they form the ultimate material atom; it is the Buddhic atom, and this ultimate material atom being formed by this, is held together because there is a certain rate of vibration given to all of them, therefore, holds them together, and, being held together in this way, the atom, this ultimate material atom, vibrates in accordance with that vibration, and then when these ultimate material atoms descend in their vibration until they come to the rate of vibration which pertains to the mental plane, they form the ultimate mental atom, by combination with the atoms which are vibrating to the rhythm of the mental plane, are thus drawn together and held together by reason of this rhythm and what is the result? Why, the vibration brings them together and they form the ultimate mental atom, or if it be on the astral plane, the ultimate astral atom; if it be on the plane of life, the vital atom; or if it be in the ether, the pure ether, the outer akasha, then it forms the ultimate physical atom. All these ultimate atoms are formed by reason of this vibration which is given to them. Now what takes place? Each one of these atoms produces a sound which is given to that ultimate atom, which is the result—that is, the sound aspect of that particular rhythm, and whether it be on the mental plane or astral plane or the plane of life or the physical plane, there is a sound pertaining to each, and each one of these ultimate atoms has its own particular sound. Were your clairaudience sufficiently developed, you would be able to hear the sound and to distinguish the different atoms, each severally by itself, as the sound of each is different all the way along.

We find that these ultimate physical atoms are brought together—that is, when they descend a little lower in the rate of vibration, they are differentiated into electricity or magnetism, and thus they combine again, being drawn together and a certain note is struck. This note is played, as it were, is sounded by this electron of electricity or magnetism as the case may be. Then again as we come on, descending, come a little lower, the electricity differentiates, it has gone into hydrogen and oxygen—that is the ether which forms hydrogen and oxygen, of course, descending from its higher form. It is rather water and fire. Then the electrons of magnetism form nitrogen and carbon, or, in other words, earth and air. These are formed as they differentiate, coming down lower. They thus come together again, being drawn together, and form atoms of the four elements of earth, air, fire and water, or, in modern parlance, oxygen, nitrogen, hydrogen and carbon. These are brought together, the notes combined and form the chord which by the combination of these notes, these four ultimate chords are formed which are the result of vibration of the various atoms, and thus the atoms each play their own chord, so that each atom is playing a chord by reason of its vibration, and let me assure you that these chords are just as definitely musical as any other chords. They are very low; their sound is reduced to the minimum, so fine, so subtle that none but a highly develped clairaudient can ever hear them, yet they are distinct musical chords nevertheless, and as a matter of fact, Pythagoras was able to distinguish forty thousand separate and distinct musical chords. A person who could do that now would be quite a musician. These chords are thus produced by the vibratory activities of the various atoms. These atoms combine in certain proportions and form eight-six different molecules, the molecule being the unit of the eighty-six elements.

When I was studying chemistry, they just had seventy-two, but there were others that could not be decided upon, and we now find that we have eight-six so far discovered. These combinations are produced by the various atoms coming together, each atom playing its particular chord, and the result is that these chords combining, form the tones of the various molecules, each molecule having its corresponding tone, and that molecule is always producing that tone, and practically the tone is composed of the various chords and the chords with the various notes. Remember, when you get so you can hear the music of the spheres in detail, you hear each of these tones and chords, and the tones are all separate and distinct. It is not a confused mass like in ordinary music because there when you have your ear sufficiently attuned, you are able to hear the entire process.

The molecules go to work to form the various bodies which we see in nature, rocks, etc., whatever it may be; the groups of matter are formed by grouping together the molecules of the various atoms. You will find that each of these bits of matter, these physical pieces, possesses its key; and this governs all these tones which go to work in fact, and thus you may take a diamond or any other jewel or piece of quartz, and you will find that it combines all these various tones together producing harmony, and it is this harmony which holds it together, and now we come a step further and we take a planet, for instance, and we find that all these forces coming together as it were in this planet, we see that all the physical pieces are held together, and this planet has a dominant note or keynote; it combines all the keys, tones, notes, chords and everything of the kind together, preserving unity, maintaining this state of unity everywhere, and what is the result? It is that the chord is preserved; it goes on accomplishing its work, and this keynote is continually being sounded and expressing itself throughout the entire planet, so this planet is playing its music as it were, within itself; but is that all? No, for the various planets in the solar system each have their respective keynotes, and the keynote, of course, is different in the various planets, for they do not all produce the same music, so that the keynotes are different, and now these keynotes all harmonize and produce a tune, and so the solar system is playing its tune; when the same tune is being played by the solar system and the other solar systems throughout the universe, each by playing its tune, and so it goes, and each tune is being produced; the various solar systems in a cluster system combine their tunes and form a symphony, which is the combination, the blending of the various tunes of the solar systems within that cluster system, and it is still perfectly harmonious all the way through, perfectly blending, not a discord present. But is that all? No, no, that is not all, for we go on and we find that the cluster symphonies combine into clusters in a group system and produce a kind of concert, which is the combination of the various symphonies, of blending together and holding together by a dominant force, so that perfect oneness, perfect unity is the result of that group system. Thus is played a concert; but is that all? No, for we find that these various groups in the grand sidereal system are combined together to form their heavenly orchestra, which produces a perfect concert which is carried on in this orchestra, and there is a grand musical production going on which is the combination of all the activities within that system. But is this all? No. Then all these grand sidereal systems are combined, and all the universe combines to form one orchestra of the universe, which includes all; and thus down through the various orchestras and concerts, right down through the key notes and the keys and tones and chords and notes and vibrations, right down, it is perfect harmony, perfect sympathy, not a discordant note, not a misfit.

We hear a great deal of talk about the universe being ruled by law. What is the law which rules the universe? It is a musical law; it is rhythmical harmony, that is what rules it. Not a discordant note ever happens; nothing can possibly happen. The rhythm is perfect, and so this music is going on. It is playing, it is working, and in this vast orchestra, planets and solar systems are the instruments; they, the solar systems, are the instruments, and the planets are the keys, the chords and strings, and thus the work is perfected in the music. Everything is the result of this perfected music and harmony. How does such perfection come about? Where is it that this is brought about? Why the motion the rhythm is producing, everything is the effect of rhythm. The greatest musical instrument in the world would be worthless unless there was a musician that knew how to play it. you have got to have a musician who knows how to play the instrument if you have the instrument. The music of the spheres therefore, touching with the whole universe, is but a musical system, necessitates a musician, a leader for the orchestra, one to govern and direct this music, and that is no doubt the reason why the materialists are so much opposed to this idea of the music of the spheres; they would not mind it if the machine could go to work and produce music without a musician, but, Oh, when it comes to having a musician who is competent to work, to guide, to control that universe, we cannot have that, not for a moment; and so what is the result? It is nonsense, superstition, charlatanism.

Now as we go along, we see that this necessitates another change of our views of nature. Let us see if that is true. Humboldt claimed that the universe was governed by fixed laws; that the course of nature was established permanently, but if the music of the spheres is true, that is not true. Every thing is the product of motion; there are definite rates of motion which govern everything. The evolution of life and form, are but the effect of definite rates of vibration. This being the case, what follows? As it is all a product of vibration, if you get the requisite vibration, you will produce the effect of that vibration, and, therefore, the only laws which govern the universe are the laws of motion, and the laws of motion, therefore, giving expression to this great universal scheme of motion, with all these so-called laws of nature are merely modes of motion and nothing more; that there is a grand force that is working back of this. Motion here is not simply confined to the physical plane, but is also operative on the astral and mental planes, and the mental atoms are moving in accordance with the motion; their activities are governed by motion. Then there is something back of intelligence— intelligent mind, instead of being the directing force of the universe, is simply one of the forces which are being moved by something else. Now what follows?s Mind is not the ultimate; there is a force back of mind, and even the activities of the Buddhic plane are moved by a force, even the activities of the Spiritual Plane are moved also.

Now, we are brought up against this proposition that the universe is a machine, kept in motion by something outside of the universe; we cannot get around it. It is absolutely an unavoidable conclusion that there is a musician outside, separate and apart from this machine, who is playing it, and thus we are forced to the conclusion of a musician maintaining it, a God who is playing, and this whole universe is merely the result of music—that which has produced it, that is all. The musician is carrying on a little rehearsal, so to speak, and the result is that his music is universal or the effect of the music, and if we recognize this, we, therefore, see the absolute necessity of recognizing God back of it all. But is that all? If this is the real cause, what kind of a God is this? If he is a God capable of playing in that way a certain set of emotions, so to speak; the music being produced acts upon the emotions and moves the astral world. What is the character of this musician? We have stated, and will state again that it is God's expression—in one sense, God's mind, just directing this whole concourse. In other words, the Mental Plane is nothing in the world but an effect of God's thinking, and the astral plane is simply the expression or effect of his feeling, and the other planes in like manner, are merely the effect of the expression of God's spirits, and thus all the way along, the seven spirits of God are expressing themselves on the seven planes of nature. It is merely this expression which starts up and maintains the motion all the way along. Then God is a God of intelligence and a God of feeling, a God of reason, Buddhi, a spiritual being, and we cannot avoid the idea of a Divine being. Merely divine force could not do this if it were simply a force; it would be an utter impossibility to realize these things because the very foundation principle of all this activity which we see in the universe is simply the activity of a being corresponding to these principles. It is back of these forces themselves. What do we have to conclude as a result of this? Simply that nature is but an expression of God, and thus, "All things are one stupendous whole, whose body nature is, and God the soul." When we realize this, we can then see how it is that the ancient Greek philosophers taught that music was the foundation of all nature, and why Pythagoras, a mystic, required that a person must be well grounded in music, mathematics and geometry before he could ever be able to enter his school, because those were the foundation; because form itself owes its origin to motion, and sound. In other words, geometry is simply a form and state of vibration, and chemistry to be utilized with the color side; music deals with the sound side; mathematics deals with the power of vibration—that is absolute mathematics, just the same as absolute music deals with the power of motion, and so we associate music with sound. However, for that matter, music can be seen as well as heard if we have the proper sight.

Now we understand the cause of the Music of the Spheres, and what it is, understanding that it is the result of the activities of all the various principles in the universe, and that motion is everywhere; therefore, we can begin to understand what a tremendous, absolute, inconceivable bit of music it must be if we could really hear it all. It sounds as if there were ten thousand different musical instruments playing at the same time, each one a little different,—but then, that is not a circumstance to what the reality is. The music of the spheres is a fact undeniable and without it the universe cannot be comprehended.

Let us see how much there is to this law of nature. Supposing the music were to be changed for one moment, a new chord with less variation were to take place, the result would be changes would take place in the course of nature corresponding to this change in the music, and the result would be that some of the laws of nature would cease to exist and some new ones would spring into being. The music will change form; God's attitude toward nature changes and as a matter of fact we know that certain cataclysms have appeared in the earth's history, and doubtless in the history of the balance of the universe which cannot be accounted for on any known process of nature, but if we understand that in the development and evolution of nature, it becomes necessary for God's attitude toward nature, to be changed by him, I undertake to say that a new force might be introduced; in other words, the music would be varied just a little so as to bring into activity, into manifestation a new force, and what would be the result? Just what did take place, and second, the researches in Geology show very clearly that these things have taken place a number of times, and instead of the universe being governed by fixed laws, there is no such thing as a law of nature. That is all imagination; that is, a delusion of the mind. The laws of nature are effects of the Divine musician's playing, and whenever he changes the music, the laws of nature will change accordingly, they are very obliging. If you looked at the music of the spheres, what would you see? If you looked at the planets you would see how a planet was composed, instead of appearing the way it does through the telescope, it would appear in a number of different pieces all the way through, different grades of matter, each separate like a structure built up, and you would see the various units, and if you were able to see a little deeper, you would see that the entire earth, the entire planet was composed of a vast multitude of molecules which were vibrating all the time through and through, simply by the form of attraction, etc., and kept in their position, and at the same time it was not solid, not dense, but simply a vast multitude, millions and billions of molecules there vibrating and held in their position, and that which holds them in position is the keynote of the rhythm.

Suppose you look at one of these molecules, and what will you see? You will see that this molecule is composed of a multitude of atoms which are also vibrating there and it really is not solid; it is merely a group in the position of atoms, held in a certain relation one to another, and it is because of the tone which holds the atoms of these molecules together; and so again we may look at one of these atoms, and we find that it is a form of electricity in some way; we will actually see this condition, we will see that it is composed of electrons, and the electrons, in turn, of ultimate atoms, physical, astral, vital, mental, which are also vibrating and maintaining their position by reason of the rhythm pertaining to it, or, rather, the note pertaining to it. We go back some further, we look at one of these ultimate atoms, being the physical, vital or mental atom, and what do we see? We see that this in turn is a structure, grouped, a kind of colony of ultimate material atoms which are vibrating in the same way, and looking at one of these, what is it? It is simply another colony, another group of the spiritual atoms, the Nirvanic atoms which go to form it, and thus what do we know when we look at them? We see that this universe is nothing but a vast ocean of energy which is bound together and held in position by vibration maintained by harmony, a perfect scale, a perfect system of the most elaborate music vibrating, and is held together by perfect harmony from the highest to the lowest gradations of vibration all the way along. Then what follows? What conclusion do we come to?

We see the unreality of so-called matter, and we see that there is nothing in all the universe but the will of God, the purpose of God, being a manifestation through nature. If you are a clairaudient, you can hear this music, infinitely beyond all comparison. Nobody can comprehend it, nobody can form the remotest idea of what it means until he has heard it, until he has seen its activities, and this is what Davis calls the Great Harmonica, which is ruling all things, visible and invisible, perfectly united, perfectly harmonious, and now when we see that all the universe responds to this motion, to this impulse, that the will of God is governing all the universe with harmony, we realize the audacity as well as the futility of man to arrogate to himself the prerogative of harmony and maintaining a separate existence from God and the universe. He refuses to respond to this music, and the result is he maintains a state of discord. Of course, he gets the result of all the discord, suffering disease, decay and death. Will he never learn to let the music of the spheres play through him? Will he never learn to become an instrument tuned to the music of the spheres? If we do this, we come into harmony with nature. Do you remember what Trine, in his book, "In Tune with the Infinite", says? What does that mean, anyway? What does it mean to be in tune with the infinite? Why, simply to let the music of the spheres play through you, to bring yourself into harmony with this music which is already formed. When you have done that, you are in tune with the infinite, there is nothing more for you to learn, you have come in touch with that which is beyond all things you know.

Let us say, in conclusion, that the music of the spheres is no dream. It may appear to be a nice piece of pleasing speculation, but it is not a speculation, for no person has ever arrived at a conception of this until he has heard it or seen its activity, not necessarily physical—no, not that, but he must first be conscious of this activity before he can philosophize on the matter, and when he has brought himself in tune, he has reached the foundation, the ultimate of human knowledge. It is the realization of this great music which is back of and which is at the foundation of everything in all the universe, and we are all effects of it, more or less.

LESSON VI.

The Rhythm of Life.

The vital force in its activity is a product of vibration. It owes its origin to a definite vibration the same as all the other forces in nature.

You must bear in mind that all the natural forces are solely the product of a definite state of vibration. All life force vibrates on that plane or the rhythm which pertains to life; the rhythm of life governs the activity of all the vital forces. Whenever the energy in its vibratory activity reaches that scale, that rhythm which we term the rhythm of life—they are drawn together—that is, the ultimate atoms are drawn together and form the ultimate vital atom. The ultimate vital atom is composed of a party of the ultimate material atoms which are held together by the rhythm of life. It is by reason of that rhythm that they are held together, and they, in all their activities, act, move, or vibrate in accordance with the rhythm of life, or the rhythm of life governs and controls their action, and there are almost infinite differentiations of that rhythm, and, of course, some vibrate much more highly than others do, but all vibrate in accordance with the rhythm of life. The more intensely they vibrate, the more of life is manifested.

The only thing which is necessary in order to transmute matter into life is to cause its atoms to vibrate in accordance with the rhythm of life. Whenever you do that, you transmute it into life or prana. The vital force, as I stated, always vibrating in accordance with life, and the tissue which is vibrating in accordance with that rhythm, must necessarily manifest a greater quantity of life.

What is the difference between living tissue and dead tissue? We hear a great deal about the decaying of live matter and dead matter. What is the difference? The difference is simply this; in living tissue, or in living organisms the tissue is vibrating in accordance with the rhythm of life, and, therefore, is manifesting life, while in dead tissue, or dead matter the rhythm of life is absent; the rhythm of death has taken its place—that is, the rhythm which is below that of life, and which, therefore, cannot manifest any vital energy.

There is a subject about which the physicists have given much attention, and that is how to generate life from matter, and with them spontaneous generation of life would all be solved if they could just find out how to impart the rhythm of life to the vibratory activity of this substance.

Whenever the rhythm of life disappears from an organism, the rhythm of death takes its place, and then decay begins, disintegration begins in that tissue. That is why a body, soon after life has disappeared from it, has left it, begins to disintegrate. What does it mean for the life to leave a body? You often hear the expression, "Life has flown." What does it mean for life to flee from the body? It simply means that the rhythm of life has ceased to act in that body.

Now you can understand, therefore, that just as long as you can maintain the rhythm of life in the vibratory activity of a body, just that long you can make a person live; just that long you can maintain life, and the moment the rhythm of life ceases to act there, death is the inevitable result.

Disease is also the outcome of the absence of the rhythm of life. When tissue has a high rate of vibration, or short wave length vibration, moving with great intensity, the molecules are never allowed to be still, they are in a continuous state of activity; the result is that the tissue manifests an abundance of life. If disease germs get in there, they cannot do anything, they cannot rest, the disease is precluded from making any progress because every molecule and atom of the tissue is in intense motion all the time, is vibrating intensely, and, therefore, it is an utter impossibility for disease, decay or death to manifest itself because the rhythm of life prevents it. As long as water is running or is in a state of agitation, it is perfectly fresh, but what takes place when water ceases to run or ceases to move,—becomes still? Pretty soon a scum forms over it; it becomes stagnant, wiggle tails appear in it. The same thing takes place when the rate of vibration in the tissue gets low; it becomes almost stationary, it becomes stagnant, disease is able to manifest itself and disease germs get in there and get in their work. There is no danger from germs,—they are absolutely harmless if the tissue is vibrating with a sufficient degree of intensity; it is only when the vibration becomes low; the wave length of vibration is long, and it takes a considerable time for it to make a revolution, to make the circuit, we may say, and the result is everything is still and torpid, and disease is able to manifest itself, to take up its abode there and do its work, but when you increase the rate of vibration to a high degree, then it is an utter impossibility because there is too much life there, and there can never be disease where the rhythm of life is present.

Old age is likewise caused by the absence of the rhythm of life; persons get old because the rhythm of life is not very active; it is low. What is it that really causes old age? Old age is caused by the settling of lime and chalk, and these salts act upon the tissues as well as the arteries so that their walls become hardened and become calcinous and lose their elasticity, and that is really the cause of old age. Whenever a man dies from old age, he dies from that cause; it is the accumulation of the so-called mineral matter. These earthly salts accumulating in the body obstruct the vital functions and the rhythm of life ceases from that cause; it is the accumulation of too much of the so-called mineral matter, this earthly salt accumulating in the system. If the vibration were sufficiently intense, it would be impossible for these salts to settle in the system; it would be kept in a state of agitation all the time so that accumulation would be impossible. Therefore, accumulation is the result of a low state of vibratory activity. The absence of the rhythm of life, is the cause of old age, decay and death.

You must bear in mind that not only is the vital force in man acting in accordance with this rhythm, but the individual prana is moving according to the rhythm. There is also a universal prana, a cosmic prana, which corresponds to the prana in man. This universal force is the same as this third principle in man.

The universe, and everything in it, is formed on the basis of the septenary principle. We have a spirit, a cosmic spirit, a cosmic soul, a cosmic mind, the mahat, and there is then the astral plane of nature as well as the astral in man, and the life force or universal prana, and the universal ether or cosmic ether, and then the physical side, the gross physical side of the universe. This is the septenary division of nature. All created nature is divided into or manifests itself upon these seven planes, and this is the macrocosm; then man partakes of these created principles, the spirit of man corresponding to the spirit of nature, and the soul of man corresponding to the universal soul or Purusha, and the mind of man or his mental body corresponding to the mental plane of nature, the astral body of man corresponding to the astral plane of nature, the individual prana corresponding to the universal cosmic prana, the etheric double in man corresponding to the ether of the universe, and man's gross physical body corresponding to the gross physical body of the universe. Man is, therefore, the microcosm of nature, of the macrocosm, or great world.

Each and every principle in man corresponds to a principle in nature. Each principle in man and also in nature, acts in accordance with a rhythm corresponding to that principle, so that the rhythm of life is not only in operation in man's prana, but also in the universal or cosmic prana.

This rhythm of life is in a state of activity, or rather, this cosmic prana is moving in accordance with the rhythm of life all the time. It is this fact, that man is the microcosm of nature, that is the basic law of astrology. Astrology really owes its truth to the fact that man is a microcosm of the universe, and so is every other portion of the universe a microcosm of the whole.

The sun and the moon and the various planets affect man because the same principle which is in man, is also in those bodies, and, by reason of their acting upon, polarizing and acting through the rhythm upon the same principle in man, they are able to influence him; not only that, but all of these bodies apply to and represent certain principles.

There is a certain principle of man and nature preeminently represented in the various planets, and it is because of this fact that they are able to exercise their influence upon you. The planets and the moon and the sun are in man, and it is for that reason that they exercise their great influence upon him.

In the exact proportion as any principle in man acts in accordance with the rhythm pertaining to it, so does it polarize with the corresponding principle in nature. Even so, and in the exact proportion as man's prana moves in accordance with the rhythm of life and the more intensely that rhythm is expressed, in his prana, even so it is polarized with the universe of cosmic prana, and thus his prana is moved in accordance with the same rhythm that the universal or cosmic prana is moved, and just as surely as he polarizes with this pranic force of the cosmos, so does he embody it.

Man's prana, therefore, is not limited except in regard to the degree to which he acts or expresses the rhythm of life, but to that degree does he draw from and embody the universal cosmic prana. That comes into him, he embodies it, and thus he takes it, and he expresses it, and there is no limit to the quantity of life which may be expressed through an organism provided you can maintain the rhythm of life at sufficiently high point, and thus you will be able to fully express the life just so far as you maintain that rhythm within your own being.

The supply of life is infinite, and consequently, by expressing that rhythm, we draw into us that supply of life, and the longevity of people, the vitality which they possess and the energy and force, are in direct ratio to the intensity with which the rhythm of life is manifested by their activity.

How is a man to embody in his own being the rhythm of life? He must, as soon as possible, take into his system only food which has that rhythm, and the water which he drinks, and everything of the kind, and there are various ways in which this can be secured, but one of the most important sources of this life energy, this rhythm, is through his food. What I mean is that not only the prana, but every cell of the human body should be vibrating in accordance with the rhythm of life.

It depends upon the substance from which this cell is built as to whether a high degree of rhythm will be manifested. Suppose you eat a large quantity of meat; the meat is that of an animal which has been killed, and an animal which is dead; from which the rhythm of life has departed, and which, if it is not preserved by artificial means, will begin to disintegrate in a very short time.

There is absolutely none of the rhythm of life secured from it, but, on the contrary, the rhythm of death is there present; therefore, a cell which is built up on that kind of tissue, will have the rhythm of death instead of the rhythm of life, and this rhythm of death will have to be overcome by life forces; therefore, it will neutralize a great deal of it, and you do not have the cell there at all.

There is no greater fallacy than the idea that vitality can be secured from meat eating. It is an utter impossibility to get a single bit of vital energy out of meat, for it does not come from heating, combustion, as many physicists think. It is solely and entirely the outgrowth of the rhythm of life; therefore, in order to have a high degree of life being expressed through an organism, it is necessary to absolutely exclude all meat or dead tissue because the cells which are built up from it will not possess the rhythm of life, and therefore, vitality will not manifest itself.

Another very important cause of low vitality is the eating of cooked food. The fruit or grain or nut, or whatever of that description, which is taken into the system, is a life organism; it has the seven principles, which is the same as man, and everything else, as a grain of wheat, or barley, a peach or a plum or an orange or anything of the kind that you take into your system has these seven principles. When it is cooked, the temperature in cooking reaches that point where the vital principle, the astral principle, which is the vehicle of life or prana, is unable to maintain its affinity with the physical and etheric principles; the result is the astral cell takes the Prana with it, and goes off on a tangent; and the same thing happens there that happens to man when the temperature becomes too high, if in a burning building, the astral simply goes off and leaves the body.

Just exactly the same thing takes place in cooking food; the astral and all the higher principles leave the body of the food, the grain or whatever it is, so when you eat it, you simply eat carcasses; you do not obtain the life; it is gone. Therefore, the rhythm of life is not there, consequently a cell built up by this kind of food does not possess the rhythm of life. It will, therefore, not express this rhythm, and consequently the other life forces must be consumed and hampered by this dead cell.

On the other hand, if the cells are built up of raw food—cereals, fruits, nuts, etc., which possess the rhythm of life, they will, therefore, as they are dissolved, impart this rhythm of life to the entire system, so that the cells that are taken out of this organism, this tissue, will possess the rhythm of life, and everything will be built up and will express this rhythm in all other activities.

The water which we drink, also, imparts a considerable quantity of prana, provided it has not been boiled. Hot water is generally supposed to be a wonderful thing, but a greater mistake never was made. Hot water will cause the prana to leave it when it attains a certain point of heat. In distilled water and boiled water and everything of that kind, the Prana is gone and it will not tend to a maintenance of the rhythm of life. Natural cold water is far the best from the standpoint of imparting vitality.

Another, and perhaps the most important method of receiving Prana, is in the breath. By breathing, we draw in a lot of Prana through the lungs, and thus the system receives it, and this Prana always moves in accordance with the rhythm of life, and, therefore, imparts that rhythm to the organism. Not only through the lungs do we do this, but at the same time, while we are breathing in the Prana through the lungs, there is a current of it rushing through the skin and through the entire body so that the entire body is drawing in Prana, and, therefore, receiving the rhythm of life.

Another point is this: by rhythmic breathing we bring ourselves in contact with the universe. The rhythm of life is thus established within us by reason of our respiration and our circulation, the circulation being governed by the breathing circulation.

When we consider that the blood circulates in rhythm, when we breathe in rhythm, we in that way acquire the rhythm of life in this Prana, into the system by reason of having this rhythm; also by thinking in rhythm, in bringing the mental activity in this way and by training the mind to act rhythmically so that we feel rhythmical, and we thus acquire this rhythm and thus we polarize ourselves with the great life force of the universe and draw it in, so that, as stated before, there is no limit to the amount of vital force which we may acquire, except the limit on the rhythm of life which is being manifested in our being, and, therefore, the limit of our capacity to polarize ourselves with the universal life force of nature.

The rhythm of life is, therefore, that principle which differentiates between life and death. If we could impart the rhythm of life to a corpse, we might see him awakened to new life and resurrect him, and that is exactly what did take place in the resurrection of the dead among the saints in times past.

Those who do not understand the rhythm of life may scoff at the idea of Christ resurrecting the dead; not only He, but others—for He was not the only one who did—but this scoffing is due solely and totally to the misapprehension of this great power of the rhythm of life. When men have learned to understand this principle they will then say that there is nothing impossible or even improbable, in any such man as Christ, actually raising the dead.

All that is necessary to be done is to set up the rhythm of life, when it can be forced in that body. He certainly knew this, and when He undertook to do it, He merely forced His great imagination upon a mental picture, and it was necessary to concentrate His mind and form a picture of the rhythm in a state of activity in this organism, and then by projecting this picture, by causing his own force and vitality to go in accordance with this picture, and then by the activity of the will, project his aura, so that it entered the corpse, acting in accordance with the rhythm of life, could be so forced as to arouse that vibration—that life vibration within this corpse, so that it began to act in accordance with the rhythm of life, and immediately the person is restored to life.

Take the case of the resurrecton of Lazarus after he had been dead four days; when we realize the man had been dead four days, and that, therefore, the rhythm of death was in a state of activity in his organism, disintegration had begun, the Master simply in the same way, applied the rhythm of life to him and caused life to manifest, changed the tissue until life manifested everywhere, and so the dead was alive. That was all that was necessary, and that was what took place.

Of course, it would require a person of a very high order to be able to get up the rhythm of life in a dead body, but, notwithstanding that fact, the resurrection of the dead is in this way brought clearly within the comprehension of the mind which understands this great law of rhythm. The healing of the sick is merely another example of the use of the rhythm of life, and such an act of changing the rhythm was performed when the sick were healed, and all those wonderful feats of healing which Christ and his apostles and the early saints performed, were performed by the sudden establishment of the rhythm of life in a high degree of intensity in that body; and inasmuch as disease cannot exist where a high degree of vibration in accordance with the rhythm of life is manifesting, therefore, to establish the rhythm of life in a high degree of activity, and establish that quick intense short wave length of vibration which manifests so much life and establishes itself in that tissue, would necessarily mean the expulsion of all traces of disease. It could not manifest under such circumstances, therefore, it disappears like frost before a noon-day sun; it was an utter impossibility for it to exist when this rhythm was manifesting, therefore, the dead were raised, and the sick were healed, and it is a manifestation and activity of the rhythm of life that is made to manifest itself in this organism.

Thus we see that life is simply and entirely a product of a definite rhythm, just the same as everything else; it is a manifestation and outgrowth of this great system of Motion and Number. Vibration of life forces, wherever it is, must cause life, and life is nothing but a vibration and moving in accordance with rhythm—the rhythm of life—and, therefore, must manifest and have expression in life. The absence of that rhythm must have caused the reverse of that, namely, death. Death, then, it has been said, is the absence of life, and that is true; and life being the result of the rhythm of life, death is the absence of that rhythm. Death is simply that condition where the rhythm of life is absent—that rhythm is not in a state of activity, therefore, disintegration and death take place. The rhythm of life produces life wherever it may be.

The Rhythm of Mind.

The Law of Rhythm reigns in the world of Mind quite as much as in the world of Life. The only difference, in fact, between the two being that the Mental vibration is on a higher Plane than that of Life. Life, or Prana is on the Astral Octave, while Manas, or Mind is upon the Mental Octave. The lowest Mental vibration is, therefore, one step higher than the highest vibration on the Astral Plane.

The student must grasp the idea of Mind separate and apart from Thought. Mind is the Material out of which Thoughts are formed. Mind is universally diffused throughout space in the same way as the ether, Prana and Astral Matter. It is, therefore, a form of Energy and not merely Thought.

The rhythm of Mind governs all the activities of this mind stuff. When the atoms of the inner Akasha, or Buddhi, i. e., the Cosmic Energy, begin to vibrate in accordance with the Rhythm of Mind, they are drawn together and held by cohesion, thus forming the Ultimate Mental Atom, the unit of all Mind Stuff.

The Mental Octave is composed of seven Notes governing the seven Sub-Planes of its vibratory activity. All mental vibration is on one of these Sub-Planes and is governed by one of these notes. A Thought is an organism, a mental-electron, so to speak, formed by the union of a number of the Ultimate Mental Atoms, governed by the same rate of vibration, giving to the Thought itself this particular vibration. A

Compound Thought is a mental atom formed by the union of a number of Simple Thought Electrons, governed by a chord peculiar to them all. A Complex Thought is a mental molecule formed by the union of several Compound Thought Atoms, governed by a single keynote. A Thought Form is a body of unorganized Mind Stuff ensouled by a thought.

Each Thought has a definite rate of vibration, is, in fact, the result of that vibration; hence it follows that there are as many Thoughts as there are vibrations on the Mental Plane. The same Vibration will in all cases organize the same Thought. The more gross thoughts occupy the lower Notes of the Octave, while the higher and finer ones are governed by the higher Notes. The higher the rate of vibration is, the higher will be the quality of the Thought, and vice versa.

In order that Thought may manifest itself to the Physical Consciousness, it must have a physical medium to offer the necessary resistance to enable it to manifest itself. The brain has been provided for that purpose. It is in this sense that the brain is the Organ of the Mind. The brain is composed of tissue so organized as to offer the necessary resistance to Thought Vibration and to nothing else. It is in this way that the Mind is enabled to function through the brain.

As the various rates of mental vibration, expressing themselves in the form of corresponding thoughts, may be grouped into classes, each class or vibration resulting in a corresponding class of thoughts, even so may all thoughts be divided into classes. The point which the student must bear in mind is that thoughts of a certain class, or quality, all have the same vibratory note. In a word, character of thought is the result of a corresponding vibratory note, hence thoughts having the same general character, have also the same note of vibration.

In order that this class of thoughts may be generated, there must be a quantity of brain tissue adapted to the expression of such vibration. In other words, unless there is some part of the brain adapted to the vibration, in such a way as to offer to it the requisite degree of resistance it will be impossible for that vibration to manifest itself as a thought. These different classes of thoughts, with their different vibratory notes, constitute the diverse Faculties of the Mind.

As each Faculty must have a quantity of the brain matter specially adapted to the expression of its particular vibratory note, in order that it may manifest in thought, it follows that different parts of the brain must be assigned to the diverse Faculties, with special adaptation to their special notes of vibration. This is the real foundation of the functional areas of the brain.

As a section of the brain becomes adapted to a particular vibratory Chord, it is for that very reason unfitted for the manifestation of any other chord. For the above reason, the existence of definite sections of the Brain for each Faculty of the Mind, is absolutely necessary. If the same quality of matter prevailed throughout the Brain there could only one faculty operate, namely that whose vibrations were governed by the same chord to which the brain itself was keyed. Phrenology is, therefore, the only possible basis of Psychology.

The strength of a faculty is determined by the length of the Brain Fibre. The fibre running from the brain cells to the brain center and return forms the circuit over which the mental impulse must pass in order to make the connection of cells, and thus realize itself in a Thought, corresponding to the impulse in the rate of vibration and, therefore, being that Impulse expressed in form.

The length of the Brain Fibre determines the strength and power of the Thought. It is for this reason that phrenologists count the strength of a faculty according to the distance of the surface of its brain area from the brain center, thus securing a fair estimate of the length of the brain fibre. This is what is meant by the relative size of an organ, viz.: the length of its brain fibre, and the consequent length of the Mental Circuit, which the impulse must make in forming the connection in order to become a Thought.

IN ORDER THAT THE MENTAL IMPULSE MAY EXPRESS ITSELF IN THOUGHT, there must be a Brain Fibre of such quality as to respond to the vibration set up by that impulse of the mind and offer the necessary resistance to enable it to manifest in thought. In a word, unless the fibre has the quality of resistance to the Mental Impulse, by the overcoming of which the vibration may be carried along the fibre to the cells, it is utterly impossible for the impulse to manifest through this particular fibre, and if there is no such fibre in the entire brain, it will be impossible, in that case, for the Impulse to manifest in thought at all. That is why so many of us are limited in the range of thought which we are able to express. It also accounts for the fact that we are constantly haunted with Mental Impulses which we are utterly unable to express in thought, but which continue to haunt us like the ghosts of ideas.

Before these haunting impulses can be expressed in Thought we have to develop Brain Fibre which is keyed to that particular Vibration. This is the real art of Brain Evolution. By the continual effort to express a certain Mental Vibration through a Brain Fibre we gradually change the quality of the same until it reaches the point where it is sufficiently sensitive to that Vibration to offer the requisite resistance to enable it to manifest in the corresponding thought.

Although the Brain Fibre may be sufficiently sensitive, or rather may be keyed to the proper vibration, so as to convey the vibratory Impulse to the surface of the Brain, yet if the cells are not keyed to the same Vibration, this Impulse will never be able to express itself in Thought. Before this can be done it is necessary that the cell be first developed to that exact degree of Vibratory Response, where it will express that Vibration.

This being accomplished, the Vibratory Impulse passes along the Fibre, making the Circuit to the Surface of the brain where the cells are brought together, the Positive and the Negative Poles uniting to form the combination necessary to the manifestation of that particular thought Vibration in the form of the Thought which corresponds to it in vibratory value.

The entire Brain is, therefore, only a complex instrument, adapted to the conveying and manifestation of the diverse vibrations, arising out of the effort of the Mind to express itself in Thought. However without this Brain it would be utterly impossible for the Mind to manifest itself in Thought, while upon the Physical Plane. And, in fact, the Mind can only act for a brief period of time upon the Higher Planes of Nature when deprived of the Physical Brain. The whole secret of Mental operation, therefore, is based upon the law that all Mental action is vibration on the Mental Octave, that each Thought is the effect of a particular Vibration, that in order for this particular vibration to manifest as Thought, it must have a Brain Fibre over which to travel, possessing the requisite degree of sensitivity to afford the resistance to convey it to the surface, and that it must there find a combination of cells adapted to the same rate of Vibration, through which it may be able to manifest itself as Thought corresponding to the Vibration which organized it.

Mind is a system of Vibration, the Brain with its Fibres and Cells is the Vibrator, and the Thoughts are the organized effect of each particular Vibration expressed through the requisite combination of cells. The number of Brain cells, therefore, has nothing whatever to do with the range of Thought which is possible to a given Mind. If the Cells are all adapted to a certain range of Vibration, they can only express those vibrations in Thought. All others either above, or below that range will be beyond the reach of such Brain activity.

The theory, then, of the anthropologists, that the breadth and power of the mind is indicated by the size of the brain, is absolutely untrue. The size of the brain only indicates the raw material which the mind has at its disposal and it must take this and adapt it to its purpose before it can be of any service, for the purpose of generating Thought. The shape of the brain indicates the range of thought, with tolerable accuracy, because it indicates the length of the brain fibre in a particular portion of the brain and, hence, the exercise which it has received, and, therefore, the relative activity of the same; and as we know the function of each part of the brain, we are able to tell with tolerable accuracy, the range of the thought of which the given mind is capable.

It is not the number of the cells, but their vibratory adaptability which counts, in giving greater range to the thoughts of which the mind is capable. It is merely a matter of rhythm, and as the rhythm is, so will the thoughts be.

The real mystery of the intellectual harmony and discord between different people, where there is no apparent cause, really lies in the rhythm of their respective minds. If they harmonize in the rhythm, all will be harmonious between them; if not, all will be discordant. It is merely a case of perfectly natural sympathy or antipathy between the two minds. Neither one is responsible; it is not a question of ethics, but one of Mental Chemistry.

Each mind has a rhythm or keynote peculiar to itself, and cannot possibly come into *rapport* with a mind which is not in harmony with that rhythm; for the same reason, it must enter into *rapport* with any mind that is in harmony with its keynote. This law of mental rhythm explains all of those problems which come under the above heads. This is why the great world of thought—which is all around us, filling the Mental Plane—does not impress itself upon our consciousness. We can receive and take cognizance only of those thoughts which have the same rate of vibration as some portion of our brain is able to respond to and, by the duplication of the same, to express in the mind the same vibration in the form of a thought.

This is the sense in which it is true that we can receive only that which we have within ourselves. We can bring into consciousness only that thought or idea which has the same rate of vibration as some of our own thoughts and, therefore, as some portion of our brain fibres and brain cells, in order that they may respond to the vibration, and thus reproduce the thought which gave rise to it in the mind.

As our Mental Horizon broadens, giving a continually increasing capacity for a greater range of vibration, we are thus able to polarize with a correspondingly increasing range of vibration of thoughts upon the Mental Plane. This gives a corresponding increase in our capacity for Spontaneous Telepathy. Capacity for reading the Akashic records, therefore, depends upon the ability of the brain to respond to the vibration of the Mental Plane, and thus bring those thoughts into our consciousness; or else, when out of the Physical Body upon the ability of the substance of the Mental Body to respond to the vibration of the particular thought.

What is herein stated in regard to the law governing the reading of the Akashic Records, applies as well to the activity of all the psychic powers upon the Mental Plane. As the Rhythm of Mind accumulates with increasing force throughout the body of a man, the Creative Energy is in ever increasing quantities transmuted into Manas or Mind stuff. Therefore, as is the degree of activity of the Rhythm of Mind, in the finer energies of the body, so will the quantity of the Manas be.

As is the quantity of the Manas in the man, so will be the extent of the Mental Body. The Mental Body is thus formed out of the Physical Body, by the activity of the Rhythm of Mind. As all thought is moving in accordance with the Rhythm of Mind, it follows that all thinking builds up the Mental Body, by increasing the quantity of its substance, the relative fineness of that body, however, depending upon the nature of the thinking, and, therefore, upon the vibratory value of the thoughts which influence and act upon the Manas.

Remember, therefore, that all thoughts alike build up the quantity of the Manas composing the Mental Body, but the quality of the Manas as well as the nature and value of the Mental Body, depend upon the nature of the thinking which is constructing that body. The Mental Type of man is, therefore, continually consuming the Physical Body in order that he may have the material from which to build the Mental Body. It is for this reason that the men of great intellectual power are invariably men of comparatively weak physical power.

Those foods which have more of the Rhythm of Mind, will be found to be far more conducive to the increased strength and volume of the Mental body than those which have less of that Rhythm. It is for this reason that certain foods have been found to be much better for brain workers than others. Raw food is much more conducive to mentality than cooked food, because in cooking, the Mental Principle, as well as the Astral, and also the Soul and Spirit leave the food, so that you eat only the Physical Principle. As a result, none of the food contains the Rhythm of Mind when transmuted into Energy.

The Rhythm, being purely physical, must be transmuted into the Rhythm of mind by the activity of that Rhythm when directed upon the same energy. For this reason it will be found that raw food will be far more conducive to the Rhythm of Mind, and, therefore, to the volume and strength of the Mental Body, resulting in a corresponding increased power of the mind, than Cooked Food. It is for this reason that meat is also very undesirable as food for those desiring to secure the best results from a mental standpoint. As the meat is always from an animal which is dead, the Rhythm of Mind is, of course, absent, therefore, it can afford only the physical Rhythm, therefore, it must be transmuted before it can be utilized by the Mental Body.

Certain foods are found to be of much more value for the mind than others. This is because their Rhythm approaches nearer to the Rhythm of Mind, and thus makes the act of transmutation correspondingly easier than in those having a rate of vibration correspondingly more remote. It is this same principle applied to the Soul and Spirit which provides the real reason for the strict Dietary Regime imposed upon Mystics and other Ascetics.

The Rhythm of Mind may also be established throughout the System, by Chest Breathing. This will aid in the development of the volume of the Mental Body.

The quality of the Mental Body will, at all times, absolutely depend upon the character of the Thinking, as the volume of the Mental Body depends upon the amount of the thinking. It is through the adaptation of the Vibration of our Mental Body to the different Rates of Vibration of the Mental Plane that we are able to Polarize with that Plane and thus to come into contact with their corresponding Thoughts through the Rhythm of Mind. It is thus that Mental advancement is made possible.

The Key Note.

In all organic bodies the various atoms, electrons and molecules are drawn together by reason of the different rates of vibration uniting into the diverse notes, chords and tones, being held together by adhesion and cohesion so as to form a body composed of thousands and millions of electrons, atoms and molecules, vibrating and revolving around each other, held in position by reason of their vibratory relation to a common center of gravity.

This principle is really the origin of all form, be it great or small. The molecules which collectively go to form a group of molecules or what we would term a bit of matter, being the compound result of the association of a number of different molecules, there is a dominant note which, by reason of its greater power, is able to dominate, control and give direction to the activities of the various notes and tones in the vibration, so that all the molecules are held in a certain relation by reason of this dominant note. This is termed the key note. It is because of the relation which the vibrating molecules have to this central dominant or key note that the integrity of any group of matter is made possible.

Were it not for the existence of this key note the molecules would, by reason of their different vibratory states, go off in a tangent and the material body would thus dissolve into the different molecules which went to compose it.

The key note is, therefore, that force which gives integrity to the material body and determines the proportion in which the diverse molecules will be associated, even determining the specific arrangement of those molecules and, therefore, determining the nature of the object that is the compound result of this molecular association.

The key stone of an arch bears the same relation to that form of structure that the key note does to all structures. It is by reason of the peculiar position of the keystone, its ability to bind together the various geometrical angles of the building so that every part of that building or arch has its particular relation to the keystone, that it is possible for such a structure to maintain its integrity. Also every building or structure of any kind possesses its key note. By discovering the key note, musically speaking, of any building, and monotonously sounding that key note on an ordinary violin, it is possible to tear to pieces the most powerful structure in the world. The most perfectly built suspension bridge can be made to fall into the water, being entirely disorganized, merely by the continuous sounding of its key note. This is made possible by reason of the fact that the continual vibration acting upon this key note, sets up the rate of vibration throughout every particle of the structure, so that every molecule of the metal is made to vibrate in accordance with the key note, until the cumulative activity of this vibration produces such an enormous force that the entire bridge is disintegrated and thus collapse takes place. Were this to continue long enough the very metal itself would disintegrate into its component molecules. It is merely by the continual stimulation and accentuation of the particular rate of vibration which this key note governs that the disintegrating power is made possible.

This fact proves that the only thing which guarantees the integrity of any structure is the key note; in other words, the dominant note which controls all the vibrations and preserves them in a certain systematic form.

The key note, then, is the very essence of form; without it, there can be no form. Soldiers in crossing bridges have found it necessary to break step because the continual rhythmic step of an army of infantrymen will in time establish such a powerful rhythm in the vibration, that the structure will go to pieces right there. This is because the continual rhythmic march over the bridge will impart to it a vibration which will be stronger than this key note; the result will be that the key note will no longer be able to maintain its ascendency and thus to preserve the equilibrium in the vibration of the structure, consequently disintegration is the result.

It is due to the key note that we have the various forms; that is to say, the difference between one object and another, is the difference in the constituent molecules and in their particular arrangement. Now, that arrangement of the constituent molecules is due absolutely to the particular key note; that is to say, to the nature of the key note which holds them in position. Change the key note and you will change the character of the object, just as if you abolish the key note you abolish the character of the object; it becomes characterless and the object, as such, goes out of existence, breaking up into its constituent elements.

It is not only rocks and buildings and objects of this character that have their key note, however, but it is also true that what we ordinarily term living objects, as well as plants, etc., have their key note. The key note of a certain plant determines the nature of that plant. What we mean to say is that the only difference between an oak tree and a mullein stalk is the difference in their key notes, and as you change the key note in a plant you correspondingly change the character of that plant. The great problem, then, in the improvement of plants is merely a problem of the improvement of the key note, that is to say, raising that until it is gradually varied, approaching a higher state. However, bear in mind that the key note cannot be entirely changed; it must simply be a variation of the key note. For this reason there is a limit to the variation of plant life. We cannot originate a new family, neither can we breed one family into another, for the reason that to do this would necessitate the formation of an entirely new key note, which is an impossibility. For this reason the Darwinian theory of evolution and the entire system of biology founded upon Darwin's theory, is a physical impossibility, necessitating as it does violation of this principle of the key note, which is the most fundamental of all the laws of nature.

In animal life we find also that the key note problem is just as powerful, just as far reaching as it is in the plant life, and not only this, but it becomes more and more complicated, owing to the fact that there is a greater degree of mind and a higher degree of emotion and greater expression of life in the animal than there is in the plant; consequently there are more factors which go to make up the key note than in the plant because, bear in mind, the animal derives its entire nature from the complexity of its key note; it is that which differentiates it from other animals. In a word, the individuality of the animal is due to its individual key note and everything which goes to make up this complex individuality must be counted as a part of the key note. What we mean by this is that the key note is merely the complex result of the diverse vibrations of the being and that the individuality is the result of this complex vibratory arrangement; consequently you must trace all the peculiar characteristics, the peculiar elements going into this individuality, back to different rates of vibration in the diverse members, corresponding to this characteristic.

In man, also we find the key note and, of course, it is much more complicated in him than it is in the animals because of the greater degree of life expression, the greater complexity of his mind, his emotions, etc. The expression of the soul and the spirit, also, must be taken into consideration, and thus we find in the human species the greatest possible variation of vibratory expression. All these diverse vibratory activities blend and harmonize in the production of a key note with such force as to hold this body together in a certain inter-relation. Not only is this true of mankind as a whole, that is there is a human key note in contradistinction to all other key notes, but races likewise have their key notes, the key note of a race being common to all of that race, being a certain variation of the human key note. Also it will be found that families have their particular key note, religious denominations, philosophical cults and, lastly, each individual has his own particular key note.

Also, bear in mind that the key note of man is continually changing, going through a continual process of variation. Every word which he utters, every thought which comes into his mind, every emotion of his heart exercises a corresponding influence on the character of his key note, the key note being the result of all the expression of his being, of everything which expresses itself in the terms of vibration, be it on a large or a correspondingly small scale.

As man grows and develops, his key note is correspondingly raised or lowered. It is in this sense that we are the product of our past thinking and action, not in any vague or mystical sense, but in the most natural and common sense manner imaginable, because our thinking and emotions, our actions, etc., move along a particular rate of vibration. They, therefore, contribute that rate of vibration to the making up of the key note.

Now, as the key note is not something stable, something permanent, is not a thing, a material object, but is simply the harmony of all the diverse vibrations, it is consequently altered in harmony with all the vibratory influences which are introduced to make it up, and for this reason, the very organism of the man and all his various principles are changed to adapt themselves to this particular key note, the result of all this being that man's whole being is continually in a state of flux, becoming the organic expression of his past activities.

We cannot, therefore, say that man has any permanent individuality, but rather it is always going through a process of construction; that his personality is merely the result of the harmonious activities of all the past vibrations and also of those which are going on at the present time, his key note giving expression to those vibrations in respect to their finished result or the result of their harmony.

We may say, therefore, that man's key note is not settled, but is always transforming itself or going through a process of transformation in accordance with his general activities, but not only this; the key note has the power of giving direction, to a certain extent, to what those activities will be.

Human progress, therefore, consists in the continual elevation of the key note, while retrogression is the falling back or lowering of the key note, so that all the members are able to function on a lower plane. As the key note is raised from one note to another on the octave, man's being is raised so that it functions on those different notes. When the key note is raised from one octave into the octave higher, the result is that man becomes conscious of things on that higher octave and so we may say that man's key note is the physical or the astral or the mental or Buddhic or the spiritual, according as his vibration has been raised, so that he practically functions there, and wherever the man's key note is there will be his greatest center of consciousness.

A family may develop a certain key note until the children are brought into life with that key note to begin with. It becomes the main or fundamental key note of that family. The individual member, then, may rise above it or he may fall below it, but all who come into that family, with few exceptions, will be found to possess that key note. It is in this way that the family key note is developed.

Also a certain community or a certain city may have definite standards of living ever kept before them until the people in that locality, by the influence which they exercise one upon another, develop the common key note. The influence therefore, is to continually reproduce this key note in that city or community.

Likewise an entire nation may develop a key note which is common to that people. The result is all the Karma which is produced by that nation will be found to move in accordance with that key note, consequently its influence upon any individual will tend to the development of that key note in that individual. It is in this way that the national type is produced, which is continually reproducing itself in the particular nation where it is found to be developed. A stranger who has none of that key note in his make-up may go into that locality, may live there for a few years and he will be found to have taken on the condition of those people, to have become the typical man of that country in spite of himself because all of the unseen influence which is around the country, all of its atmosphere, mental, moral and spiritual influences, the emotional influences around there are moving in accordance with that key note, consequently anyone placing himself under those influences must embody the key note likewise. This is really what is meant by the genius of a certain locality. It is not that it is some great, wonderful ghost which dominates everything, but it is the key note of that place, the dominant note governing all the vibratory influences and which must, therefore, affect every person who comes in contact with it. This is the great secret of the force of environment. The environment which influences man is not the economic conditions or the force of example existing around him; it is not the environment which we would see from a physical standpoint, but it is rather the invisible environment, that environment which we cannot see, but which works in the subtle realms— the key note, in other words, which has been developed and exercises its subtle influence and brings about the change. It is in this way that buildings have an influence on the people who come into them; it is because of the key note which they have built up and possess. It is for this reason that it is best that a building should be used for a definite purpose. A church should be used for nothing but religious worship because in so doing it will build up a key note which will dominate the vibration, religiously, of every person who goes into the building. Whatever a building is used for it should be used in such a way as to build up a key note which will correspond to that use, and by so doing we will find the greatest results will be achieved.

One of the best illustrations of a national key note, which is to be found is that of Egypt. The ancient Egyptians have so thoroughly permeated the atmosphere of Egypt with the influences emanating from them that the key note of Egypt is purely Egyptian, and possesses the power of transforming every being or every person who comes into the country so that he is gradually being transformed into the old Egyptian type physically, which is the expression of the inner life of the people. The modern Egyptian has been built up from the ancient Egyptians, the Persians, the Greeks, Romans, Vandals, Saracens, the modern Arabs, Turks, French and English and yet, after a family has lived in Egypt for three generations you cannot tell them from the ancient Egyptians. Even the cranial formation of the Egyptian is becoming precisely the same as that of the mummies, showing conclusively that the thinking, the feeling and everything which moulds the formation of the physical is dominated by the key note of ancient Egypt. Lord Cromer when he went to Egypt was just like any other Englishman—a typical Englishman. After thirty

years his complexion had changed; the color of his hair and
eyes—his entire make-up, until he had become almost a
typical Egyptian.

In America also we find that the people are becoming more
and more of the type of the Indian; not by intermixture.
Those who have kept their blood perfectly pure for a few
generations are developing the character and the features
and everything, to a great extent, of the American Indian, il-
lustrating the power which the key note of a country has in
moulding the people who live there into its own expression.

Bear in mind, therefore, that the key note is the harmonious result of the diverse vibratory activities and that the
key note of the environment will have the influence of bringing the key note of the individual into harmony with itself;
that is, it will dominate the individual's key note in such a
way as to control the vibratory activities. When this has been
accomplished the result will be the complete domination of all
the vibratory activities of the human constitution to conform
to the activity of the key note with the result that man will be
seen to take on those influences, being moulded into that particular form and character.

The key note, then, is the very essence of man's personality, and by the proper controlling of this principle it is
sometimes possible to absolutely dominate our own evolution,
evolution being merely a process of gradually altering the individual key note. You may take a musical instrument and
play on it until you strike a man's key note. When you have
done this, by sounding that note gently and slowly you will
find you will be building up, strengthening the person. You
can play new strength, vitality, energy into a man's being.
On the other hand, by running very rapidly, running away
with yourself, so to speak, you can set up such a vibration of
antagonism, such harmful vibrations and keep it up until the
man will go entirely insane if he cannot get away from that

sound. It is merely a process of controlling the vibration of the entire being. When you become too rapid, the vibration is disintegrated, while if it is slow and regular it has the power of building up and strengthening the being.

The key note is, therefore, the essence of all organic existence on any plane or in any degree of intelligence, be it in the mineral, vegetable, animal or human kingdom and the key note is merely the dominant note of vibration. It has the power of holding together the diverse vibrations in their proper relation so as to bring harmony out of these different vibratory states; therefore, the integrity of any organic body or of any being is purely and solely a question of the vibratory rates in the being and of the harmony resulting from their compound association.

We find, then, that all existence is merely the result of vibration harmoniously associated. Were it not for this principle, the binding, uniting, blending and harmonizing of vibration so that instead of going on a number of different lines in opposition, they are brought into unity through the action of the dominant note or key note, there would be no such thing as organic being, the organism being the mere outgrowth of this harmonious blending of vibration. The key note is the means of bringing about this state of harmony no matter on what plane of nature it may manifest.

The Esoteric Meaning of Color.

As all vibratory activity expresses itself in form, color and sound, it follows that the energy is always of that particular color, shade or tint which belongs to that particular rate of vibraton. This is true not only of those colors, shades and tints which are perceptible to visible sight, but also of the finer forces of nature which transcend the physical senses.

All energy of whatever quality is continually vibrating at some rate and, by reason of this vibration, it assumes the color, shade or tint belonging to that specific rate of vibration.

As the quality and value of all forms of energy is due to their rate of vibration, it follows that the color, being an indication of the rate of vibration, will also indicate the quality of the vibrating energy.

It, therefore, follows, that we have the foundation for an exact science of chronology, even implying the psychology of color as well as the chemistry of color. When we see the color which energy assumes we can recognize its rate of vibration and, therefore its quality and value. This being true, it is possible to classify, occultly speaking, all matter and energy of whatever degree of perfection, or imperfection, according to the color which it assumes.

It should be borne in mind that the color of a visible object is due to the rate of vibration of the molecules and atoms composing it and, therefore, the value of this object may be distinguished by its color, the same as the value of energy in a state of diffusion.

It may occur to the student's mind that this would not be true of substances which had been dyed. The student may think that when a garment or anything else, for that matter, is dyed, it assumes the color corresponding to the dye, without reference to its vibratory activity, but there he will be mistaken. The dye is only able to dye the fabric because of the fact that it is composed of certain chemicals which will set up a vibration of the kind belonging to them and will change the vibration of the substance which is being dyed. Dyeing, therefore, is not simply a matter of painting or anything of that kind, in the sense in which it is ordinarily understood, but it is really a question of bringing about a chamical change in the constitution of the substance being dyed. It must, in fact, bring about a change in the rate of vibration. This is the reason why there is so little accuracy in the art of dyeing. It is known to dyers and has been known for a long time that dyeing was a very questionable practice so far as its results were concerned. We can never be sure of what the result is going to be—whether the cloth will give the color intended exactly or not. Now, the reason why this is so difficult is because we cannot always tell just how hard it is going to be to change the rate of vibration in the fabric, so as to make it conform to the vibration of the color we have in mind. It is for this reason that special dyes must be made for silk, wool, cotton, linen, etc., the same dye being not suited for all kinds of substances. Not only is it true that different kinds of cloth require special dyes; it is also true that wool will dye much more deeply than any kind of cloth. In fact, the sole problem of dyeing becomes plain when we realize that dyeing simply consists in changing the vibration of the substance until it corresponds to that of the dye.

Then the whole problem of color is a problem of vibration, and colors divide and subdivide themselves according to their occult value. We must, therefore, go into color chemistry in order to understand the problem of color.

Let us first take the primary colors. These are red, blue and yellow. All the other colors are combinations of these colors in certain proportions. Red is the physical color and is the color of all physical energy. There are various shades of red, of course, which have their various significations, but generally speaking, red is the physical color.

The color of ether is pink, or, more literally speaking, the color of a fresh-blown peach blossom, although its vibration is so intense that very few people are able to see the vibration; but ether is always pink.

Crimson is the color of affection and human feeling. It is the self relative color because our affection is given to persons on account of their particular relation to us. Affection is purely a physical and animal feeling. It is not one of the high and noble emotions that it has generally been supposed to be, but is purely animal in its character, pertaining solely to the physical nature of man, therefore, the color which it produces is crimson, the color of blood, because it is through this blood relation that we have this outgrowth of affection.

Scarlet is the color of anger, the color which the astral body of man assumes when he is in an intensely angry condition. Now, anger is really the forcible action of the will in a very positive manner moving outward, acting from the center of the being outward. This is what produces the state of anger. It is also related to the physical. In anger we feel our whole repulsion rising against the physical body of the object of our anger, just as in affection it is the drawing of the physical. We cannot have affection for a person's soul, neither can we have anger at his soul. Both these emotional states are related to the physical nature, therefore, it is always red.

Red is also the color of the Will. Wherever the will is expressed it assumes the red color because Will is the outflowing or manifesting principle, the extension or presentation of the Self into manifestation; therefore, it is the same truth expressing itself in and through the physical; it must, therefore, bring about a vibratory tendency toward physical expression. Consequently it becomes the color of red.

Rose is the color of life, the color of the prana, and as we approach toward the physical it is more red; that is, the highest degree of physical life is red. As the life is brought under the influence of emotion it, of course, takes on the blue color, and whatever color is found to be blended with this red or rose color, will indicate the presence, in that degree, of that particular color. Also, it should be borne in mind that the paler shades indicate a corresponding weakness of that particular principle, accompanied by a corresponding preponderance of the spiritual principle, which is white, while the darker shades indicate a presence of the black element, the element of destruction, disintegration—the material, evil, etc.

The second primary color is blue, the color of emotion, the color of the astral body and of the astral plane. In fact, all astral matter, that is to say all energy vibrating on the astral octave, is blue or red according as it is the positive or negative aspect, blue being the negative, feminine or magnetic side of astral matter, while red is the positive, masculine side, the will, in a word. The bluer the matter may be, therefore, indicating the absence of the red, the more magnetic it is, while the redder it is, the more electrical it may be. Will and Desire are thus the two poles of astral matter, Will being red, Desire blue. The dark blue indicates the more material desires, the pale blue the more spiritual.

It should be borne in mind that these colors are not simply a sign as a form of symbolism to represent those emotions, etc., but on the contrary, in their very nature, those emotions, when active, will vibrate at such a rate as to naturally take that color.

Indigo blue is the color of occultism and the dark indigo partakes of the evil, the element of sorcery to a certain extent, the left hand power, while the pure indigo is emblematic of pure occultism.

Violet, being a very high rate of vibration, is the color of Magic because it is so far above the ordinary rate of vibration that it has the power of neutralizing and even transforming those rates into its own, thus giving the power of alchemy and other magical activities.

Purple, being blue mixed with red—therefore, the positive aspect of emotion,—astral matter positively expressed,—is the color of mastership, and when seen in the aura of a person, always indicates the master.

Lavender, that is, a pale purple, a great deal of white mixed with purple, indicates the master on the astral plane, but merging toward the spiritual—a highly spiritualized aspect of purple, in fact.

Pale azure blue is the mystic blue, indicating the union between the astral body and the astral world and also, as it becomes paler, indicating a union between the astral and the spiritual. The paler the blue becomes, no matter what shade it may be, lavender or any of the other shades, in fact, the more of the spirit is indicated, while the darker it becomes, the more of the evil is present.

The third primary color is yellow and is the color of the mental plane. By this we mean that all the mind states, the Manas are some shade of yellow. Everything vibrating on the mental octave is yellow. The darker the yellow the more evil the more gross and material is the character of the thought; the lighter it becomes, the more spiritual it is. The clearer the yellow is, the more purity of thought, that is to say mind without any foreign intermixture is indicated; but, on the other hand, if it is muddy and without this clearness, it will indicate the mixture of foreign elements. The brighter the yellow, the more intense and pointed, the more brilliancy of mind is indicated, while the duller it is, the less of this.

These remarks apply to all the other colors on every particular plane as well as to the yellow.

The mental body which is formed of the four lower notes of the mental octave, corresponding to the region of concrete thought, is some shade of ordinary yellow, that is to say, neither gold nor primrose. The darker the shade is the more it approaches the material, and any mixture of blue in with the yellow would indicate the mixture of astral matter.

The three higher notes of the mental octave, the region of abstract thought and their microcosm, the causal body in man, are either gold or primrose, the lower note usually being gold. Pale gold indicates the same as this only a more spiritual aspect and these two colors relate to things in themselves, to absolute truth in a way; the pure absolute truth, however, the impersonal truth.

The highest type of Manas is indicated by primrose yellow; it is the pale primrose which indicates that mental attitude when the personality has been entirely obliterated from the consciousness. The presence of red in this indicates also, the rising of the will and its relation to the physical as well, to the external expression.

Above the mental plane we have the orange octave which is the Buddhic or soul octave. Orange is formed by a combination of yellow and red, in almost equal proportions.

Buddhi or determining intelligence, is really the Will working through mind; not the astral will, of course, but the Buddhic Will, but it is mind expressing itself outward and expanding, going out of its own particular circuit, its little sphere and uniting itself with the universal. It is, in a word, the individual mind uniting and blending itself with the universal, just as in the universe it is this going upward toward the spiritual, the ever-expanding Manas, but in this expanding it becomes Buddhi and is no longer Manas but determining intelligence; therefore, orange is the color Buddhi, of all the substance of the Buddhic plane and of man's Buddhic body or soul likewise.

The more positive expression of Buddhi, pure reason, is more red, while the negative aspect, intuition or indrawing, feminine principle of Buddhi is less of the red.

White is really the combination of all the seven colors. They are all found to unite in forming the white ray. The seven prismate rays unite to form this. We can prove this by the prism. The prism has the power of breaking up the white light into the seven prismatic rays, therefore, white light is really the combination of those rays.

White is the color of the spirit and it is known that all the various planes of nature are really but differentiations of the spirit. As the physical energy and the life force and astral matter and manas are all manifestations on different scales, different octaves of the Buddhic substance or cosmic energy, even so that is simply spirit, Atma, on a lower octave.

As all the colors are included in the white, so is all matter included in spirit and is but an emanation of spirit.

Gray is formed of white and black. We might express gray as being a kind of dirty white. It, therefore, indicates the mingling of the white spirit with the black.

Black is the reverse of white. White indicates the spirit. Black is the opposite pole, therefore, it indicates the extreme of materiality; not materiality in the sense of physical substance, but materiality as the antithesis of spirit or the disintegrating force; as spirit is going forth into manifestation on the lower scale, and matter comes back to spirit by being refined and separated and black indicates that disintegration which leads to annihilation in a sense, and this gray is the spiritual vibration with a certain degree of vibration of disintegration, destruction, blending with it and working in conjunction with it, through and through.

Pearl gray is, owing to its darkness, one of the most material of all the gray shades, while silver gray is the highest, being almost white and also indicating something finer than white, the presence of the silver which we will study in a moment.

White is the color of the individual spirit, not the universal spirit in the highest sense of the term; that is, the ordinary white is not. If it have a mixture of different shades, that particular shade will indicate its value. Now, the presence of any other color would indicate the blending of that force with the spiritual color or the spiritual impulse, operating through the white. A yellow tint imparted to the white would indicate mind working in conjunction with spirit. Thus, we find that cream is really a little yellow mixed with white and, therefore, it indicates an intellectual aspect of the spirit. If there be blue mixed with the white, such as a certain shade of milk, for instance, it will indicate the astral working through the spirit. The snow white will indicate that which has separated from the other principles the pure spirit, almost.

That form of white which is ordinariliy denominated pure white, is without any other intermixture in any sense whatever, and, therefore, indicates the pure individual spirit.

There is, however, a finer and higher shade of white, which we might denominate fleece white. This indicates the universal spirit, while the Divine spirit is represented by that shade of white which we speak of as being White like the Pure Wool, of the very finest fleece without any deviation from this whatever. This White like the Pure Wool is the color of the Divine Spirit. There is still a higher color than this, namely, Silver, which has a certain brightness added to the white and puts it on a still higher plane.

The highest of all the white colors is opalescent, the color of molten glass, which is the color of the very being of God Himself. Particularly when there is evidence of fire present in this opalescent color, then it is just as high as it is possible for the most perfectly developed clairvoyant on the very highest spiritual plane to distinguish any color; therefore, when St. John speaks of the Sea of Glass mingled with Fire, he is using the nearest expression which it is possible to employ to express the very highest spiritual perfection.

Green is the color of action. It is expressed by minor chords, and is the positive expression of the inner being as expressed through action. Unselfish action—action which is purely altruistic in its character, which has no relation whatever to the individual, is a clear emerald green, and the nearer this approaches to the spiritual, the paler it becomes.

The livid green is the color of jealousy. We speak of people being green with jealousy, and we speak most appropriately. It is really an indication of green whenever we see jealousy. And why is it that people become jealous? Obviously it is because their action is in reference to themselves. They feel that the person is not treating them right and they put forth their individuality into action. The self acts because they do not feel that they have been treated right, and because of this feeling, this state of jealousy is produced, for jealousy is, in the last analysis, the expression of self love.

Brown is, in a sense, a mystical color, in that it indicates the presence of white, red and black in certain combinations and possibly also yellow. According as the shade is, so will its influence be.

We must bear in mind that any combination of these colors will draw its meaning from the interpretation of the diverse colors which go to make it up. Not only should we bear in mind that those energies on those different planes and the corresponding parts in the human constitution have that color; that all vibration on the particular rate, octave or note will assume that particular color, but also that any substance of that color is sending forth vibrations of that particular quality; consequently any garment or anything else of a given color is vibrating continually and sending off an aura which is vibrating in accordance with the character of the energy which assumes that color.

By wearing garments of the particular color, therefore, we will be able to stimulate those principles which correspond to that color. Blue stimulates the Astral body, yellow the Mental body, gold the Causal body, orange the Soul, white the Spirit, rose the Life principle, pink the Etheric Double and the physical body, etc. Green stimulates us to action, black will bring on death and disintegration. It also stimulates the evil; and everything that we have said of the various colors applies here to their effect for the purpose of stimulating the corresponding principles in the human constitution and all of this must be related to its efficiency from the standpoint of practical occultism.

Color is, therefore, one of the manifestations of vibration and all vibration manifests in corresponding color, the color being merely an indication of the occult chemical activity. Therefore, we can distinguish by the color the quality and value of any chemical substance by reason of its particular rate of vibration, and all objects of any particular color have that vibratory activity and vibratory value which pertain to that color. As the color is, so is the vibration. Sound and form are no more the expression of this pure harmony than is color. Just as the form which, expressed in the Cosmos, is the creation of motion, so is the color of all its component parts.

The Building of the Cosmos.

It has been observed that all elements, chemicals, etc., have as their unit a definite geometrical figure peculiar to themselves. There are no two chemicals, the unit of which is the same figure. For this reason, it is possible for assayists to recognize any mineral by microscopic examination, the process being merely to examine the mineral through the microscope, observing the form of its unit or crystal and thus identify the mineral.

It is, therefore, due to the fact that the crystal of each mineral or chemical whatever kind it may be, has a form peculiar to itself, that such assaying is made possible.

If you will go through the entire realm of nature, you will find there are no two chemicals, the crystal of which is the same. The crystal of frost is altogether different in shape from that of every other substance; so likewise the crystal of gold or silver, of salt, sugar, snow, ice, everything of the kind. We see, then, that the crystal of each and every substance is a definite geometrical figure, and any bulk of that chemical is consequently merely a structure built up by the assembling of a number of those units. The nature of any chemical may, therefore, be ascertained by an inspection of its crystals. As this is true, it, therefore, follows that the crystal formation is due to the same cause by which the nature of the chemical is due.

What we want to ascertain is the principle in nature which gives rise to the form of the crystal and thus, also, to the character or nature of the element being crystallized. When we have learned the secret of form, we will have learned the secret of the identity of all objects.

Sir William Crooks in his experiments with sand has given us the key to the building of the crystals. He took some very fine sand and scattered it over the head of a drum. Then, by taking a tuning fork and sounding different notes just above the drum head so that the vibration set in motion by this particular key or this particular note would vibrate upon the drum head, the sand was seen to shift and assume a definite geometrical figure, corresponding to the particular key which was sounded. Whenever another key was sounded the sand shifted and assumed another figure, demonstrating that the keys of a musical scale will in their very nature, produce a certain form corresponding to them, in any substance sufficiently plastic to assume a form under their direction. This experiment may be followed *ad infinitum*. It will be found that for each note, key chord or tone of music that may be expressed, the sand will assume a corresponding geometrical figure different from that produced by any other.

This, therefore, proves to us that vibration is the origin of form, each particular vibration giving rise to a corresponding form.

Music, then, is at the foundation of physics and this is exactly what was taught by Pythagoras and the peripatetics. The universe was built by music; that is to say, harmony. We must differentiate between pure harmony, absolute music and what is ordinarily denominated music. Form, color and sound are inseparably connected with all vibratory activities; that is to say, these are the three-fold activity of absolute music, which is the activity of vibration. Each vibration expresses itself in a form corresponding to that particular rate of vibration. It is because the various chemical elements, so-called, are the result of energy vibrating at a certain rate that the crystal is formed in this particular form; that is to say the form which is the natural outgrowth of that particular rate of vibration.

Form, then, is the organized result of energy at a certain rate of vibration. We see, then, how that vibraton expresses itself in a corresponding geometrical figure and in this way builds up a crystal which is the formal expression of that vibraton, a number of these crystals collectively forming a body of the particular elements which is the outgrowth of that particular vibration. Not only the origin of form, but the origin of the divers elements is, therefore, traceable to vibration.

Vibration, then, is the source of all organized life, activity, being. It is also the source of all chemical differentiation and the origin of every form. Not only is this true of physical matter but it is also true of matter on the higher planes. The clairvoyant is able to see music as it comes from the instrument, vibrating through the ether and in each case there is a definite geometrical figure assumed by each note, chord, tone, etc. Not only is this true, but you can tell the music of one composer from that of another by examining the forms which it takes in its activity as it rises from the instrument. Wagner's music does not produce the same form as that of any other composer, being of a much higher order than that of most—more spiritual, expressing itself, therefore, in those forms which are most expressive of spirituality.

It has been observed by the students of nature that the crystals are never seen to be exactly alike. Not only is this true of the different chemical elements, but we know further that each individual crystal is a little different, a slight variation. Now, knowing that this crystallization is due to vibration and all differences in the form of the crystal are, therefore, due to differences in the rate of vibration, we can recognize the fact that the individuality of any object, that is the crystal which goes to form the object, is due to the corresponding individuality in the vibration which gave expression to it.

The universe was built by vibration; that is to say the specific form which everything has, on either a large or small scale, is due absolutely to the specific rate of vibration which gave expression to it. The universe, then, both in general and in particular, is the effect of a system of vibration; in other words, the music of the spheres, has expressed itself in that form which we denominate the Cosmos. Cosmos, meaning in a general way, the order of things, is the order of arrangement which the vibrating music of the spheres has assumed as the form through which it is expressed; in other words, the Cosmos is organized by the action of the energy vibrating in accordance with certain rates which express themselves in that particular form and cannot possibly express themselves in any other form. The universe, could, therefore, in no case be anywise different than it is unless the vibratory influences which organized it had been different, the universe being the expression in form of those vibratory influences which have organized it out of the Cosmic energy.

Inasmuch as the universe is the expression in form, of the vibrating energy, it follows that there has been a fixed purpose guiding the vibration of those energies; otherwise the result would have been chaotic. We would not have the orderly arrangement in form that we have were it not for the fact that there has been a guiding intelligence which has caused all the vibrations to move in harmony so that the form would be harmonious, systematic in all of its arrangements. It is the expression of the Divine spirit, through harmonious vibration which, in turn, acts upon the cosmic energy, causing it to vibrate in harmony and thus to become organized into the form which we see manifested in the cosmos.

The universe, then, is nothing more nor less than the

organized expression of the activity of God's spirit in matter and inasmuch as the universal form is perpetuated year after year without any great deviation, it follows that the vibration is practically the same. There have been no sensible alterations in the rate of vibration in the cosmic energy. For this reason the vibration continues in its regular path perpetually reproducing itself in form. The universe is stable for the reason that the regular and orderly course of vibration is kept up and as this is the reflection, as it were, of the perpetual activity of the divine spirit, that in turn, must keep up a regular and orderly course of vibratory activity, and if this is true, it follows that this Spirit, being dominated in all of its actions by the Divine mind, feeling, will, etc., is but the expression of the attitude of God toward all manifesting existence. The doctrine of emanations is, therefore, proven to be true. The laws of nature have no existence as permanent, irrevocable, immovable principles; they are merely the mental attitude of God, the Absolute, toward the manifested universe, and the common course of things, which is the only true meaning of nature, is merely the usual, regular and common attitude of God, and this attitude may at certain times, be slightly altered, resulting in a special activity of God's spirit,—what we would term a miracle.

What we want to call to your attention, is the fact that the universe is the organic effect of God's attitude toward the external. It is, in a word, the outer expression of the Divine Being and expresses itself in that way which is most in accordance with His designs.

Everything being the expression of his Divine vibration, it follows that every vibration must express itself in a corresponding form, so that we are not to look upon God as being the sole governor of the universal form, although He is, of course, the prime cause of it and the one who has given it its general form, but as there are other beings who think and feel and, therefore, are sending forth vibrations of certain rates, and, in fact, as everything from man down to the lowest form of life is, in its own way, expressing life along those lines, some in a very small degree, some in a greater degree of intensity, nevertheless each and every one contributing his word; and as all this activity is expressing itself through vibration, and as all vibration must manifest in form, we see, therefore, that each being is contributing its share toward the universal form; that is to say there is a vibratory influence which, to a certain extent exercises the power of emanation upon the universal form; so that the universe is not exactly what the Divine Architect designed it to be, it being interfered with, to a certain extent, by all those beings who are not in harmony with the original designs.

There is, therefore, perpetual warring between the architect of the universe and all those beings upon the universe who do not act in perfect harmony with the Divine architect. The universe, therefore, must suffer the effect of this conflict, must continue to endure the conflict until such time as the conflict is over. There is not a thought of hatred, envy, jealousy, doubt or any other of the improper attitudes, but what expresses itself in a corresponding form and contributes an influence toward marring the form of nature. We should, therefore, realize that our idle thoughts and imaginings, all our emotions are really creative; that they are expressing themselves in form; that they are generating chemical substances on the mental and astral planes which in time must descend and manifest themselves on the physical plane. We must understand that the mental and emotional attitudes of the people dwelling upon the earth will have the effect of generating plant and animal life and minerals, which are their effect; that all the higher activities of the diverse planes of nature must perpetually manifest themselves in corresponding form, and, therefore, in elements or beings deriving their nature from that particular vibration.

The whole universe, then, in whole and also in each of its parts is seen to be the expression of vibration, through form.

We have, then, in the universe crystallized music and nothing else. The whole form of the cosmos is nothing but a structure built up of billions of diverse units, crystals, which are each the embodiment of corresponding rates of vibration, those rates of vibration being the expression of the activities of the higher planes. It is, in a word, the result of a vast orchestra, of which every being in the universe of whatever degree of intelligence, great or small, is a player, and the Architect of the Universe the Grand Director.

The statement that all nature is a symbol is, therefore, seen to be absolutely true. It is a symbol not simply in the sense that it stands for and may represent to our understanding certain principles, but in a deeper and larger sense that it is the expression in form, of the vibratory activities which proceed from those forces; that those forces which are said to be in the subliminal realm, descend and cause the energy to assume the form corresponding to them in their vibratory relation to this organizing of the cosmos, which is the expression in form of those subtile vibratory activities which are descending from the diverse beings, both God and the humblest creature; so that we have, through music as expressed through universal harmony, the secret of the building of the cosmos. It has been this principle which has been at work throughout the ages as the instrument in the hands of the builders of the cosmos, in order that it might be constructed; in order that instead of chaos, we might have universal cosmos as the outward form of the subjective activities of all life.

LESSON XI.

The Fourth Dimension of Space.

The great difficulty which we have to contend with in presenting the idea of a Fourth Dimension of Space is the fact that all of our conceptions of things have been built up from the standpoint of three dimensional space; that is to say, all of our experiences in the past have been secured through our relationship to three dimensional space. We cannot, therefore, conceive of any other dimension of space, a dimension which is neither length, breadth or thickness, but which is represented by a line drawn at right angles to each of the other three dimensions.

The physical plane is limited to three dimensional space—length, breadth and thickness. On the plane of physical conciousness we have no conception of any other dimension. It is only when we rise to the higher states of consciousness that we can recognize the fourth dimension.

Now, remember, the fourth dimension is represented by a line drawn at right angles to the lines represented by length, breadth and thickness. When we see a cube, for instance, placed on the ground, we know that this cube has four sides, yet we can see only three dimensions. In a word, we see the outside of the object, but because one side is at the antipodes of the other, it is consequently invisible to us, the cube being opaque, there being four sides to the cube, in the sense in which we are now speaking, although, of course, there are six surfaces. We can see only three of them because to see the other it is necessary to look through the object, and three

114

dimensional sight will not enable us to render an opaque body transparent.

In order to enable the student to grasp the principle involved in three dimensional space, it will, perhaps, be advisable first to imagine a straight world where there is but one dimension of space, namely length. A person dwelling in a straight world, being possessed of one dimensional sight, would, therefore, see everything in straight lines. He would be absolutely incapable of seeing or cognizing breadth or anything except length, because he would be unable to recognize or see anything except in the terms of straight lines. He would, therefore, be unable to form any conception of a second dimension to space.

Again, suppose one rises above this one dimensional space and rises to two dimensional space. He lives in a flat world. He is able to see length and breadth, but not height. He cannot recognize one line as being above another, although he is perfectly able to cognize a number of parallel lines or even cross lines. He can see two lines, of course, but not a third line; that is to say, he cannot see one line or one plane above another. When he rises to the third dimensional space, he comes to the world as we have it now. He, therefore, will be able to recognize height, length and breadth, but he cannot yet see the fourth dimension.

The Fourth Dimension of Space is a dimension at right angles to length and breadth as well as thickness. In other words, three dimensional space takes cognizance of the surface of things.

Now, what would be the point which would be at right angles to length and breadth as well as thickness? Evidently the center of the object. Imagine yourself in the center of a cube and you can readily see that you will be at right angles to every point on that cube's surface.

Fourth dimentional space, then, consists in the ability to

place one's self in the center of an object and to see every part of that object in its relation to every other part. What is it which will enble a man to place himself in the center of an absolutely solid body and view every part of that body at right angles to himself? Bear in mind what we have learned in the past, that all objects are made up of molecules; no matter what the form is, it is a multitude of molecules. Now, if you can see those molecules separate and apart from one another, if you can feel them, if you can come in connection with the molecules, you will thus be able to present yourself, as it were, in the center of the object, or at least, to see through the object. The object is opaque to third dimensional sight because we see it as a whole. To fourth dimensional sight it becomes transparent, because we take cognizance of the separate molecules, being able to examine them in detail. The molecules are held together by affinity by reason of the diverse rates of vibration going on within them. These molecules, vibrating in accordance with the key note of the object, are held in a certain relative position.

Now, the dimensions of space are, in reality, the effects of vibration. For instance, length is due to a backward and forward rate of vibration; that is, the molecules vibrating in a certain direction, having a pendulum motion, so to speak, traveling in straight lines. One direction of vibration, then, or one current, produces the line. A flat surface is the result of two intersecting or cross-secting lines of vibration, forming a cross, so that we have the square. The cube is the result of three dimensions; that is to say of these two lines of vibration, with a third line going up and down; in other words, two horizontal lines of vibration, intersected by an upright or perpendicular line of vibration.

It can be seen, therefore, that what makes the object the shape it is, that what produces this three dimensional form, is molecules vibrating in three different directions. When you place yourself in the center of this vibrating mass, you have thus brought yourself into a position at right angles to each of the vibrating currents. Thus you deal with the molecules rather than with their collective result.

True, fourth dimensional space is found only upon the astral plane, where all the diverse rates of vibration are found to operate in such a way as to place the seer in possession of a perfect comprehension and sight of the molecules in any object, while, of course, the atoms and the ultimate atoms and the astral atoms as well are, to a certain extent, seen but vaguely, as it were, but the molecules in any object—and not simply the physical molecules, but also the astral molecules—are possible of clear and perfect analyzation, just as much so as the physical object itself is upon the physical plane.

It is true that when etheric sight begins to be developed we can see through opaque objects; that is to say, we can see the molecules, not individually, but collectively. If you look through an object, you can see it, but get a looking glass perspective of what you see on the other side. Everything is inverted, just as when we watch the reflection in a mirror. Getting this looking-glass perspective, of course, we see everything backwards; in a word, we have rendered the object transparent, but we do not see everything in its proper relation; we see the collective result rather than seeing the molecules individually, and thus look at them with a view at right angles to themselves.

To make the matter clearer, with etheric sight we see through the object; we are still on the outside, but it has become transparent. But on the astral plane, we are, as it were, in the center of this object; we see every point from that position. We are at right angles to every point, so that, as it were, we are present with each molecule by means of this vibrative law.

The Fourth Dimension of Space, therefore, is obtained by reason of vibration; vibration being, in reality, the fundamental key to all dimension, in fact, the creator of each dimension. When we have attuned our aura, therefore, to that particular rate of vibration, we become conscious of the vibrating body, not simply the accomplished result.

When the clairvoyant awakens to astral sight at first, he does not recognize solid bodies as such. They do not seem to him to be anything. With his sight, he sees right through them; he sees the molecules and consequently they do not appear to him as being solid bodies. He is likely to try to go through a brick wall without realizing that he cannot very well do it in his physical body because the astral body can pass through any such body as that, the molecules of the astral body passing right in between the molecules of the physical body and he, seeing from this standpoint, that is, seeing with the astral sight, does not recognize the inability of his physical molecules to pass through in this way; consequently he does not take notice of the fact that it is a solid body, and he is likely to get hurt.

Likewise, in fourth dimensional space we do not recognize the distance of the ground from us, for instance, or the distance of physical objects, because they do not appear as physical objects. Being made up of molecules and vibrating, they do not appear to be any more dense than ether, and as ether is, relatively speaking, omnipresent, we do not take cognizance of distance; but in time, when we have acquired the capacity for measuring those relations, studying them with greater care, we awaken to a realization of their true relation, one to another.

It is not to be understood that the Fourth Dimension of Space is merely a symbol, a figure of the imagination or anything of this kind, and used as an illustration; for fourth dimensional space is an actuality, it is vibration which is inward with relation to all points on the surface. It is this dimension, which is at right angles to every point and not simply to every point on the surface, but is at right angles to every molecule of this object. Now, when we realize that each molecule in an object must necessarily be at right angles to every other molecule, by reason of its vibration, we can see then, that when we cease to be, as it were, apart, and are able to identify ourselves, through vibration, with these molecules, that is to say, to vibrate in a state of attunement with each molecule so that it is, as it were, one pole and we the other, vibration passing between the two, we are thus brought into a position at right angles to the diverse molecules of that object, consequently we have arisen to the Fourth Dimension of Space. From our point of view, the astral is now solid matter—opaque. The physical has become transparent. The physical is no longer a unit, but is a heterogeneous multitude of molecules, consequently, we see through it; it has become nothing, as it were; it does not appear as a solid any longer, but in our consciousness it is simply this great mass of vibrating molecules and, we might say that, in a certain sense on the true astral plane, we also penetrate the molecules, so that we are dealing with the atom in one sense. We do not, as it were, see through it as we do in etheric sight, but we are, as it were, identified with each molecule by reason of harmony of vibration in our aura, because the same vibration which is going on in that molecule is going on in us, and to do this we must even see the molecule in relation to its component atoms and when we have seen that, in relation to those component atoms, we will be enabled to get a grasp of Fourth Dimensional Space.

Fourth Dimensional Sight is possessed in its entirety upon the astral plane only; that is to say, it is the sight of man's astral body, when functioning on the astral. This other limited sense in which it is possessed, this limited degree of Fourth Dimensional Sight, is, of course, when the etheric double is functioning.

Now, of course, when man is functioning on the astral plane, he realizes something which is really true, really existent. He becomes conscious of the force which is back of physical matter, which gives expression to physical matter. He is seeing something which has been going on all the time before he saw it; he simply has never awakened to that power of sight to perceive this force, this vibrating energy, this vibrating activity, which is expressing itself in those physical objects, and that is the Fourth Dimension of Space.

To awaken to the astral plane is, therefore, to awaken to capacity for the cognition of Fourth Dimensional Space and when we have accomplished this, we have realized a sight which is at right angles to length, breadth and thickness. Understand, we cannot see something which did not exist separate and apart from our sight. In a word, it is the impression which vibration leaves upon our sight, upon our consciousness, which gives rise to that sensation which we term sight.

Fourth Dimensional Space exists, therefore, separate and apart from physical or even astral sight—any other sight, for that matter. It is that force which is back of the organization of molecules and solid bodies.

To awaken the Fourth Dimensional Sight is to awaken into a realization of those vibratory tendencies which are expressing themselves in form. All bodies which are formed of atoms and molecules are, therefore, the three dimensional expression of the Fourth Dimension, namely vibration. Fourth Dimensional sight is the awakening of the perception to a cognition of that vibratory force which is back of the three dimensions and expresses itself through them or in them. The Fourth Dimension of Space is consequently seen to be the cause, the creator, as it were, of the three dimensions. It is in this sense that the three dimensional physical plane is but the shadow, the reflection of the Fourth Dimensional Astral Plane.

LESSON XII.

The Fifth Dimension of Space.

The Fifth Dimension is represented by a line drawn at right angles to all the other four dimensions. It must be borne in mind that the three lower dimensions of space deal with the surface of things; the four higher dimensions, with the internal side, the inward or interior of things, consequently we must find in the Fifth Dimension a line drawn at right angles to all the other four lines, and it is represented by a point inward from the other four dimensions.

It may at first appear to the student that this is an impossibility, as the Fourth Dimension is inward itself—represents the interior of things. But this is not true when we come to the Fifth Dimension. The Fourth Dimension is inward from the other three, but outward from the Fifth Dimension.

To illustrate: In the Fourth Dimension we go inward from the surface of an object; we go in to that point which is inward and from which we go into the organization of the object. In a word, the Fourth Dimension deals with Molecules. It is that molecular dimension which is the foundation of the structure and is, therefore, inward from every point of the structure. In the Fourth Dimension you are within the object, but you are external to its constituent molecules. You are, therefore, dealing with the molecules as objects external to yourself, just as in three dimensional space you deal with those objects as being external to yourself. You are living among the objects around you. On the Fourth Dimension you

121

are in the objects, as it were, but you are dealing with the molecules.

The force which enables you to deal in this way, with the molecules, is vibration, vibration as we showed in the last lesson, being that force which causes the molecules to express themselves by movement in such a way as to build up a form, a symbol possessing length, breadth and thickness, that is, three directions of vibration, each in right angles to the vibration which is expressing it to ourselves.

In the Fifth Dimension we penetrate the molecule itself; we place ourselves as it were, in the very center of the molecules themselves; that is to say, we are now living among its atoms. We are thus occupying a point at right angles to each of the constituent atoms of that particular molecule, consequently we are inward from every point of the molecule. Being at right angles to it, we have arisen to the point of atomic vibration in contradistinction to molecular vibration.

Now, inasmuch as it is this atomic vibration which constructs the molecule, the course which the atoms assume in their vibration, building up the length, breadth and thickness of the molecule, and at the same time imparting to it its particular rate of vibration—the length, breadth and thickness being the three lower dimensions, and its specific molecular vibration being its Fourth Dimension,—this Fourth Dimension is the result of the diverse rates of vibration of different component atoms.

It is only on the Mental Plane that this Fifth Dimension exists; that is to say, it is only through our Mental Body that we are able to get in touch with the inner being of any object, to place ourselves into that close touch with it so that we can be conscious of its vibration and with the force back of this vibration, our Mental Body permeating the object, as it were, blending with it on this plane which gives rise to the vibration of the molecule coming forth out of the atomic vibration.

Bear in mind that this is not simply a mental condition; it is a state of activity which exists in the object itself, separate and apart from any impression which it may have upon our consciousness, but just as the physical sight is unable to take cognizance of molecular vibration, even so, the Astral Sight is unable to take cognizance of atomic vibration; it requires Mental Sight.

It is only, therefore, by our mental faculties, the faculties that is, of our Mental body, that we are able to sense this atomic vibration which is going on within the molecule, which is the very creative force of that molecule. The Mental Body is able to see, to identify itself with the inner being and life of the molecule, so that it becomes conscious of all those vibratory activities. We enter, as it were, the molecule, placing ourselves into that state where we partake of the activities within the molecule, making ourselves for the time being a part of the object, going through its experiences. Thus we get an experimental knowledge of an object. Instead of simply watching it as a spectator, as we do on Fourth Dimensional Space, we get that experimental knowledge which comes through co-operation with the object. We attain to a certain state of fellowship with this object, in a word.

It may occur to the student to ask what is the difference between this and Fourth Dimensional Space, as it was shown that Fourth Dimensional Space was vibration and it does not seem that the Fifth Dimension is anything but vibration. Well, there is vibration and vibration. Fourth Dimensional Space, generally speaking, deals with Molecular Vibration, while Fifth Dimensional Space deals with Atomic Vibration, and inasmuch as the form or expression through length, breadth and thickness is the product of Molecular Vibration, even so, all Molecular Vibration itself—that is to say, the vibration of the particular molecule—is the expression of the Atomic Vibration.

Now, as vibration is the Fourth Dimension, that dimension inward from length, breadth and thickness, which expresses itself in a three-fold form, even so is this Fifth Dimension inward from vibration, that is, molecular vibration, occupying a point at right angles to the same and expressing itself in that way.

The FIFTH DIMENSION OF SPACE is, in fact, the Will within nature and it is through the individual will that we are able to come into a realization of it.

In order to bring this principle to the consciousness of the student, it will perhaps be best to first study it from the point of view of the individual will. Now, as a matter of fact, there is a difference between will and desire. They are both vibratory states, that is to say, they are vibratory states of the aura. The aura is set to vibrating by reason of the mental picture. It vibrates in accordance with that picture, having that particular rhythm pertaining to the picture, but there are two directions in which the aura may vibrate; the vibration may pass inward from the outside world, the external vibration may act upon the aura so that that wave is carried inward from the surface and we embody that which is without, or the impulse may start from the within—an original impulse may begin coming out of the picture and flow outward, moving through the energy of the aura and expressing itself on the world without. Thus, it may be either a positive or a negative vibratory state. In either case it is the vibration of the aura, the only difference between the positive and the negative being that in the former the vibration is from the center outward, thus active, manifesting, expressive of that which is within, or, in the case of a negative, inward, receptive, being acted upon, embodying that which is without, external.

The Will is this positive manifesting, outflowing state of

vibration. It is by means of an activity of this kind, that is to say, the outward expression of the aura that we bring ourselves into the molecule, we bring ourselves into that, place ourselvs as it were, in connection with those atoms, so that being now within the molecule, no longer influenced by its molecular vibration, no longer taking notice of it—for we vibrate with it—we have placed ourselves in this sense within the molecule; we are now acting with its atoms. Vibrating with them, we see things, to a great extent from their point of view. Instead of inspecting from without, we are co-operating; we get a state of fellowship with them and see everything largely from their point of view as one of them.

Now, this atomic Vibration is the will of the molecule, that is to say, it is flowing outward and manifesting. This is the manifesting principle, the manifesting vibration, whereas the molecular vibration is the manifested vibration; it is that which is the effect of this volitive force, this will vibrating, which is the manifesting cause.

It is in this way that we say the Will in Nature is the Fifth Dimension of Space, just as the individual will is the Fifth dimension of that individual. It is on the Mental Plane because it is only when we rise to the Mental Plane that we can take notice of this state of being. It is only at this time that it becomes possible for us to realize the truth in regard to this great Fifth Dimension.

That vibration, consequently, which expresses itself in organic form, that which we term Molecular Vibration, is the outward effect of the will, or Atomic Vibration, which is an outflowing from the center, and, therefore, the Atomic Vibration or the Will in Nature, is that point inward from, at right angles to Molecular vibration.

It will clarify the matter, perhaps, to touch briefly upon the Sixth and Seventh Dimensions of Space in order to show wherein they differ from the Fifth Dimension and to show the close resemblance between them. We do not propose to go into details here, but simply to touch upon them briefly in order that the pupil may understand the difference between these dimensions.

Let us say to begin with, that the Sixth Dimension is the Desire Principle in Nature, just as the Fifth Dimension is the Will. Remember what we said a bit ago about the difference in the positive and negative vibrations. Now, inasmuch as the Will is the outflowing, manifesting course of vibration, arising from the vibratory impulse set up in the center and moving outward until it manifests itself upon the surface, even so, Desire is the negative vibration, the vibratory impulse which moves inward from without and until it is able to express itself in a vibratory impulse in the center.

Now, this Desire Principle must take place first before it can express itself in an outward vibration. In other words, we must have an impulse brought into the Within before it can manifest itself in the Without.

Now, through this Sixth Dimension, we place ourselves, as it were, in the center of the atom, or, in other words, we draw this atom into our very being, as it were, we draw it within us so that we incorporate it, so to speak, embody it, and by bringing it into ourselves, we feel just as it feels, and taking it into our being, we are able to sense its vibration, that is, the vibration which builds up the atom. We thus get back of the atom into these ultimate atoms which build it up. In other words, we are now able to deal with the Mental, Astral and Physical atoms. We have reached that, in fact, which is back of the lower atoms, namely, the Buddhic Atom; consequently, the Sixth Dimension is only on the Buddhic Plane and is capable of realization through the Buddhic Body only.

It is this principle, then, this vibration through the Buddhic

Plane which moves inward from the Buddhic to the spiritual atom, building up the Astral, Mental and Physical atoms from the Buddhic. It is this vibration from the Buddhic which merges into the very being of the atom—which is, therefore, at right angles to the atom, thus giving the Sixth Dimension of Space, which can be realized on the Buddhic Plane only.

The Seventh Dimension of Space must be represented by a line at right angles to the Sixth. It must be that principle, which expresses itself through the Sixth.

Now, desire is the indrawing sensation or motion resulting from an idea, a picture. You form in your own mind a picture and immediately the rate of vibration corresponding to that picture is awakened in your aura. It depends, however, upon whether the Will or Desire principle is acting as to whether that vibration moves inward or outward; even so, the Mental Picture represents the Seventh Dimension of Space. It represents that state where you bring yourself into touch with the spiritual atom, the spiritual principle which expresses itself through the Buddhic, the Buddhic representing the Desire or Inflowing, embodying principle and the Mental representing the outflowing Manifesting, Will principle. Now, when you have brought yourself into this state you are thus identified with the spiritual atom. You no longer contain it within you, neither are you contained within it as in the Sixth and Fifth Dimensions of Space, but you have passed beyond that stage and through this picturing process, it is absolutely identified with yourself. You see it absolutely as it is; you go through its own experiences—perfect identification which is secured only upon the Nirvanic Plane and through the Nirvanic Body. Thus the Nirvanic is able to completely identify himself with everything with which he comes in contact and to go within the ultimate material atom, and to see, to get at right angles to the diverse parts of the ultimate atom. He is, therefore, as it were, identified with, is within the ultimate Nirvanic atom. He is, therefore, at a point at right angle to matter. He has risen beyond matter, being at right angles to matter, he being the positive pole whereas matter is the negative. He is, therefore, expressing himself in matter; he is, therefore, the creator, as it were, of matter, representing the attitude of the creative spirit, the manifesting spirit. In a sense he is on the plane of the Manifesting Brahman when he has attained the Seventh Dimension of Space. In this state man is able to come into conscious realization of the very nature of things.

The Seventh Dimension is, therefore, represented by the highest vibratory state, which is at first at right angles to the Desire state of Vibration of the Sixth Dimension, it being at right angles to the Will vibration or the Fifth Dimension, which is, likewise, at right angles to the formative vibration of the Fourth Dimension.

It will then occur to the student that these four higher Dimensions are simply four different stages of vibration; consequently, he may think they should all be included under the head of the fourth Dimension, but if this be his idea let him stop and consider that length, breadth and thickness, the three dimensions of the Physical plane, are simply three different directions in which vibration moves; consequently the three dimensional world is simply the expression of the vibration of the fourth dimension; therefore, he should, to be consistent, say there is only one dimension, namely, Vibration.

The dimensions of space are relative; they are simply the effects of vibration viewed from different points of view, so in the ultimate there is but one dimension and in the pure ultimate, there is no such thing as space; it is all an illusion. But in the relative, which we must view in our concrete activities, it should be borne in mind that there are these seven dimensions, that is to say, they are as true, as real as anything else in this world of illusion, this Maya, where nothing but God is, in reality, existent.

The directional vibration, which gives expression to the three dimensional space, is, therefore, the effect, the reflection of the pure vibration of the Fourth Dimension, this, in turn, this formative vibration being merely the effect of the descending, manifesting vibration of the Fifth Dimension, which is likewise, the effect, the manifested result of the embodying, involving vibration of the Sixth Dimension, this likewise being the effect of the Creative, originating vibration of the Seventh Dimension.

To clarify the matter, let the pupil bear in mind that the Seventh Dimensional vibration is the point of emanation; the Sixth Dimensional Vibration the involutive; the Fifth Dimensional vibration the evolutive and the Fourth Dimensional vibration the result of this evolution, this evolving process or type of realization; and the Third Dimensional Space, the work which it accomplishes. If he can hold these explanations in mind, he will be able to ascertain a fair conception of the Seven Dimensions of Space, the seven-fold manifestation of vibration, which is the foundation of all space and of all formation.

OCCULT GEOMETRY
by A.S. Raleigh

This book, first published in 1932, is "a course of private lessons given to his personal pupils." Dr. Raleigh explains and interprets symbols, which he called "nature's universal language." He shows how "God geometrizes" to produce the universe and man, and points out that in understanding himself, man understands the universe. Symbols discussed are: the circle, the line, the triangle, the cross, the swastika, the diamond, the pentagram, the hexagram, the seven-pointed star, the cube, the sphere, and squaring the circle.

Paper, 80 pages

Published by
DeVorss & Company
P.O. Box 550 - Marina del Rey, CA 90291

CPSIA information can be obtained
at www.ICGtesting.com
Printed in the USA
BVHW061756300121
598874BV00008B/625